UNDERSTANDING FAITH

Understanding the Baha'i Faith

UNDERSTANDING FAITH

SERIES EDITOR: PROFESSOR FRANK WHALING

Available

Understanding Christianity, Gilleasbuig Macmillan
Understanding Judaism, Jeremy Rosen
Understanding Sikhism, Owen Cole

Forthcoming

Understanding Buddhism, Perry Schmidt-Leukel
Understanding Hinduism, Frank Whaling
Understanding Islam, Cafer Yaran

UNDERSTANDING FAITH

SERIES EDITOR: PROFESSOR FRANK WHALING

Understanding the Baha'i Faith

Wendi Momen

with

Moojan Momen

DUNEDIN ACADEMIC PRESS

EDINBURGH

Published by
Dunedin Academic Press Ltd
Hudson House
8 Albany Street
Edinburgh EH1 3QB
Scotland

ISBN 1 903765 50 1
ISSN 1744-5833

BRITISH LIBRARY CATALOGUING IN PUBLICATION DATA
A catalogue record for this book is available from the British Library.

Set in 10/12pt Plantin with Stone Sans display
by Makar Publishing Production, Edinburgh.
Cover design by Mark Blackadder.

Printed and bound in Great Britain by
Cromwell Press

Contents

Introduction

This book is an attempt to describe a religion that is relatively young in terms of the age of humanity and therefore does not have the depth of history that religions such as Judaism and Hinduism have. Nor is it concentrated in any part of the world and so it has not built up a culture that can be described, in the way that Sikhism has. This does not mean, however, that it is easy to describe the Baha'i Faith. Indeed, anyone trying to find out something about the Baha'i Faith by searching, for example, on the Internet will find it being attacked on conservative websites as a liberal religion that is a bedfellow of communism, globalism and libertarianism, whilst other sites portray it as being narrow, conservative and reactionary. And so one can be forgiven for being completely bewildered when trying to form an idea of what the religion is about.

We have attempted to find a way to present this religion in a manner that is simple enough to be understandable to those who know nothing about it and yet avoids the simplifications of adjectives such as 'conservative' and 'liberal' which distort the picture and render it unrecognisable to its adherents. As with any portrait, however, and in particular one that is confined to a limited number of words, it must necessarily present the subject from a particular viewpoint and thus miss out on viewpoints that would have shown up other aspects of the subject.

As the above intends to demonstrate, the Baha'i Faith is not easily captured by simple descriptions. One of the main problems in presenting the Baha'i Faith is the fact that, perhaps because the religion is focused on and centred around the concept of unity and oneness, all of its aspects are themselves interconnected and bound up in an all-encompassing unity. The mystical aspects of the religion are interconnected with its administrative framework; the aspects of its teachings that relate to the individual are intimately connected with the aspects of its teachings concerning society and the global situation; its view of the physical and spiritual, the scientific and the religious, the personal and social is that these are all interdependent and aspects of one reality. Thus to try to analyse by breaking the religion down into its component parts is, to some extent, to distort it. Nevertheless, in order to write a book, it is necessary to start at some point, recognising that at whatever point one starts to describe the religion, one finds oneself needing to refer to aspects of it which have not yet been described.

This unity and interconnectedness mean that aspects of religion that in most faith traditions are considered personal and private, such as prayer and devotions, are linked to personal transformations in the individual's life through the development of spiritual qualities such as love, justice, patience and detachment, and this in turn needs to be reflected in one's social life through one's interactions with others. Thus the community also needs to reflect these qualities and these qualities also need to emerge at national and international levels. Part of the reason why the Baha'i Faith is so difficult to classify and also why contradictory opinions about it abound is the fact that what it is trying to bring about is so radical. Those who describe it as conservative and traditional are looking at the surface and observing that the Baha'i Faith holds to many of the moral values of traditional religion. Those who describe it as liberal and globalist are also looking at aspects of it that portray those qualities. But the fact is that the Baha'i teachings envision a radical revolution of human life at all levels. At the personal level, the individual must fuse the spiritual and the social in such a way that each feeds off the other to bring about the development of that person. At the social level, a radical change is envisioned that overturns the present hierarchical power structure of human society and replaces it with a new basis for human interactions. At the international level, it anticipates the evolution of a new global society in which the interactions of peoples and nations are based on justice and equity, rather than wealth and power.

Since the book is designed to be read in whatever order the reader wishes, it is necessary to introduce here at the start the main figures whose words are quoted throughout this book. Further historical information on these figures will be found in Chapter 8.

The founder of the Baha'i Faith is Baha'u'llah who lived in the 19th century. He began his life in Iran (Persia), but for most of the time that he was giving out his teaching he was in exile in what was then the Ottoman Empire, first in Baghdad (now in Iraq), then in Istanbul and Edirne (now in modern Turkey) and finally in 'Akka (now in Israel). Baha'u'llah's major teaching was that all the religions of the world have been in essence one continuous thread that has been the mainspring of human development. These religions have been inspired by a common source and have each taken humanity forward in its development. Each was brought to humanity by a specific founder and relates to the needs of humanity at a particular time.

Baha'u'llah claims that the message that he has brought is the latest in this series of messages and is particularly relevant to the present needs of humanity. Its central focus is on global unity, as Baha'u'llah teaches that human development has now reached the stage when humanity needs to put aside its differences and come together as one global community.

Baha'u'llah appointed his son 'Abdu'l-Baha to explain and expand on his teachings after his own death in 1892. 'Abdu'l-Baha brought the Baha'i Faith to the West and during his ministry, which lasted until 1921, the Baha'i Faith was established in many parts of the world. 'Abdu'l-Baha expanded on his father's teachings, drawing out their implications in terms of the problems facing humanity. 'Abdu'l-Baha in turn appointed his grandson Shoghi Effendi to be the Guardian of the Baha'i Faith, a role that involved being the authorised interpreter of the teachings of Baha'u'llah as well as leading the Baha'i community in its development. During Shoghi Effendi's ministry, which lasted until 1957, the Baha'i administrative structure was established and the Baha'i Faith was spread to most parts of the world.

Since 1963 the head of the Baha'i Faith has been an elected council, the Universal House of Justice. Baha'u'llah deliberately left his religion with only a framework of laws with which to regulate itself. The Universal House of Justice is charged in Baha'u'llah's writings with not only leading the Baha'i community but also introducing new laws as the needs of humanity change with time.

In the last few decades the Baha'i Faith has completed the task of spreading to all countries of the world and Baha'is are now engaged in developing the implications of Baha'u'llah's teachings both within the Baha'i community and in relation to the world at large. The Baha'i Faith is a religion that has been in a constant state of development and evolution since it started and a book of this size can only give a snapshot of its present state, without going into any great detail of how it got here. The organisational principle we have used for this book is how the Baha'i Faith is lived by the Baha'is themselves, in their own lives, their homes, their communities and in the wider world.

1
The Spiritual Life

The Baha'i Faith teaches that there is an interconnection and even what may be called an inter-penetration between the physical and the spiritual. Every aspect of human life on this planet is seen as permeated by the spiritual. Thus, when it comes to surveying the Baha'i teachings on the spiritual life of the individual, it is necessary to look at such matters as prayer and meditation but also at the way that the laws of the Baha'i Faith, its community structure and even its buildings impact on the spiritual.

The first question that must be answered, however, is the eternal one of 'who am I?' Human beings have two natures according to the Baha'i teachings: a physical nature, which is determined by the human body, and a spiritual nature, which is determined by the soul. In their day-to-day lives people tend to be dominated by their physical nature because it makes immediate demands upon them. They become hungry, so they find food to eat; they become tired, so they sleep; they become cold, so they seek warmth. The problem is that however much these demands are satisfied, they do not result in lasting human happiness. However much food a person eats, she becomes hungry again after a few hours; with whatever luxuries a person surrounds himself, finer luxuries always seem to beckon in advertisements; however fine the clothes that are worn, a new fashion comes along. People are endlessly chasing a mirage that promises happiness if they were only to wear the latest clothes, drive the right car, put on the best perfume or go on the ultimate holiday. The Baha'i teachings regard these activities as pursuing the needs of the human being's animal side, which can never satisfy him for long because they neglect the other aspect of a person's nature, the spiritual side.

According to 'Abdu'l-Baha, this spiritual life is the true reality of human beings; it is what distinguishes the human being from the animal. The true source of lasting human happiness and contentment consists in developing the spiritual side of the human reality. Human beings, however, do not understand this spiritual side of themselves very well. People can gain knowledge of the physical world through their senses, but how does someone gain a knowledge of the spiritual world? In human history it has been the function of religion to provide

It may be that a man who has every material benefit, and who lives surrounded by all the greatest comfort modern civilization can give him, is denied the all important gift of the Holy Spirit . . . It is indeed a good and praiseworthy thing to progress materially, but in so doing, let us not neglect the more important spiritual progress, and close our eyes to the Divine light shining in our midst . . . Only by improving spiritually as well as materially can we make any real progress, and become perfect beings. ('Abdu'l-Bahá, 1967, p. 63)

human beings with knowledge of the spiritual world. The founders of the great religions of the world have taught that if individuals do certain things it will cause their spiritual development and if they do other things it will result in their spiritual harm. The founders of religions provide the knowledge and the practices that will help individuals to develop the spiritual side of their human nature. Therefore, according to the Baha'i scriptures, people need, first and foremost, to turn to these sources of guidance and to carry out whatever practices and laws they have given.

God, Humanity and Religion

The Baha'i teachings state that the purpose of our life on earth is to come to know and to worship God. But how can a person come to know God when the Baha'i scriptures also emphatically declare that it is impossible for human beings to know God, that 'no mind nor heart, however keen or pure, can ever grasp the nature of the most insignificant of His creatures; much less fathom the mystery of Him Who is the Day Star of Truth, Who is the invisible and unknowable Essence' (Bahá'u'lláh, 1983, p. 62).[1]

Baha'u'llah states that any image of God that people have is a creation of their imaginations and is therefore subjected to the limitations of their minds – it cannot be a true conception of God the infinite. Thus the concept of the Ultimate Reality, whether this be God in Judaism and Christianity, Allah in Islam or the more abstract notions of Brahman in Hinduism, Dharmakaya or Nirvana in Buddhism, or the Tao in Chinese religion, are all human attempts to encompass what cannot be encompassed.

Human beings can obtain some knowledge of God through contemplating the physical world, which embodies some of the attributes of God. Baha'u'llah says that every created thing has been endowed by God with some of His attributes: 'Upon the inmost reality of each and every created thing He hath shed the light of one of His names, and made it a recipient of the glory of one of His attributes' (Bahá'u'lláh, 1983, p. 65). Therefore by studying nature, individuals can come to know something of God. However, Baha'u'llah goes on to add, 'Upon the reality of man, however, He hath focused the radiance of all of His names and attributes, and made it a mirror of His own Self' (Bahá-'u'lláh, 1983, p. 65). This is why the Baha'i scriptures speak of human beings as 'the highest degree of materiality, and at the beginning of spirituality', as 'the last degree of darkness, and at the beginning of light'; that the human being 'has the animal side as well as the angelic side' and that 'if the divine power in man, which is his essential perfection, overcomes the satanic power, which is absolute imperfection, he becomes the most excellent among the creatures; but if the satanic power overcomes the divine power, he becomes the lowest of the creatures. That is why he is the end of imperfection and the beginning of perfection. Not in any other of the species in the world of existence is there such a difference, contrast, contradiction and opposition as in the species of man' ('Abdu'l-Bahá, 1981, pp. 235–6).

Baha'u'llah teaches that humanity was brought into being as an act of love on the part of God and that God has imprinted upon the human soul the potential to develop all of the attributes of God. These attributes are within each person but they need to be developed. Everyone is capable of becoming loving, just, patient, wise, generous, forgiving and so forth but they need to follow the teachings and obey the laws of the founders of the world religions in order to transform this potential into actuality. Whereas in former times it was only a small number of mystics who followed the path of spiritual development, this is now the privilege and obligation of all.

The best pathway to knowledge of God, however, is through the founders of the world religions because they not only act as intermediaries between the physical world and the spiritual world, bringing to humanity the teachings of God, but they manifest in themselves perfectly the attributes of God, such as knowledge, love, justice and patience; therefore in the Baha'i scriptures they are called the Manifestations of God. In an analogy found in the Baha'i scriptures, they are like a mirror reflecting to humankind the image and the light of God. They include Abraham, Moses, Buddha, Krishna, Jesus Christ, Muhammad and Baha'u'llah, as well as others.

These Manifestations of God are the founders of the world religions. The purpose of these religions is to be a mechanism both for the refinement and growth of the individual's personal, inner, spiritual self and for the transformation of the social, collective life of humanity (this chapter focuses on the first of these). According to the Baha'i

> The door of the knowledge of the Ancient Being hath ever been, and will continue for ever to be, closed in the face of men. No man's understanding shall ever gain access unto His holy court. As a token of His mercy, however, and as a proof of His loving-kindness, He hath manifested unto men the Day Stars of His divine guidance, the Symbols of His divine unity, and hath ordained the knowledge of these sanctified Beings to be identical with the knowledge of His own Self. Whoso recognizeth them hath recognized God. Whoso hearkeneth to their call, hath hearkened to the Voice of God, and whoso testifieth to the truth of their Revelation, hath testified to the truth of God Himself. Whoso turneth away from them, hath turned away from God, and whoso disbelieveth in them, hath disbelieved in God. Every one of them is the Way of God that connecteth this world with the realms above, and the Standard of His Truth unto every one in the kingdoms of earth and heaven. They are the Manifestations of God amidst men, the evidences of His Truth, and the signs of His glory. (Bahá'u'lláh, 1983, pp. 49–50)

scriptures 'the purpose of religion is the acquisition of praiseworthy virtues, the betterment of morals, the spiritual development of mankind, the real life and divine bestowals' ('Abdu'l-Bahá, 1982, p. 152). The Baha'i vision is that the world should be a God-centred, united, peaceful, globally functioning organism, where each individual is enabled to develop his or her own potential – materially, spiritually, intellectually and emotionally – to the highest degree, and in which people are valued individually and collectively for the unique contributions they can make to the greater good of the whole. If a religion does not promote this, if it becomes a source of hatred and divisions, then the Baha'i teachings maintain that it would be better to be without such a religion.

Since these Manifestations of God all perform the same spiritual function in the world – that of bringing divine guidance to humanity – they can be seen as being the same spiritual reality that has come to the world at different times and in different places. Baha'u'llah teaches that each of these Manifestations has two realities, spiritual and physical. At the spiritual level, they are all one and the same. At the physical level, however, they each have a different name and a specific historical context. Thus, in scriptural prophecy, for example, when the term 'return' is used – as, for instance, in the 'return of Christ' or 'return of Krishna'— it is the return of that same spiritual reality that is being referred to. But each return occurs with a different name and its own historical circumstance. It is in this context that Baha'u'llah claims to be the fulfilment of the promise found in the scriptures of all the world religions that at some future time a further figure will appear: the future incarnation of Krishna, the Maitreya Buddha, the Messiah or the return of Christ.

The question then arises that since these Manifestations of God are all the same, and since they come from the same source, God, why have there been so many of them, resulting in religions that disagree and are in conflict? The answer that Baha'u'llah gives to this question is that each Manifestation of God has come with teachings that are relevant to the state of humanity at a particular time and place. Humanity has developed socially through the ages and the teachings that are relevant at one stage of this development become no longer relevant at a later stage, when new teachings are needed and a new Manifestation of God appears. In the Baha'i scriptures this is likened to the successive teachers that a child encounters at school, each of whom builds upon the teaching of the previous one and takes the child on to the next stage of its development. It may also be likened to the successive chapters of a book or to a physician who prescribes one remedy for a patient at one time but a different one on another occasion, when there is a different illness. The teachings of the latest Manifestation of God help humanity more than those of previous Manifestations because they are more suited to the present and they are available in a purer form.

> The Prophets of God should be regarded as physicians whose task is to foster the well-being of the world and its peoples, that, through the spirit of oneness, they may heal the sickness of a divided humanity . . . Little wonder, then, if the treatment prescribed by the physician in this day should not be found to be identical with that which he prescribed before. How could it be otherwise when the ills affecting the sufferer necessitate at every stage of his sickness a special remedy? In like manner, every time the Prophets of God have illumined the world with the resplendent radiance of the Day Star of Divine knowledge, they have invariably summoned its peoples to embrace the light of God through such means as best befitted the exigencies of the age in which they appeared. (Bahá'u'lláh, 1983, p. 80)

Spiritual Practices and Spiritual Development

The pursuit of spiritual development is something that an individual must train himself to attend to daily. One of the laws that Baha'u'llah gives is that the individual must pray every day. Baha'is are to choose one of three obligatory prayers to say daily as a minimum. Baha'is have numerous other prayers and supplications in the Baha'i scriptures which they use in preference to spontaneous prayers, believing these to be more powerful spiritually. These other prayers can be said at any time that the individual feels a need to pray. Baha'is believe that in prayer a person's attention is turned away from the physical world and towards the spiritual; he converses with the Beloved, God, and establishes a connection with Him, and through prayer the balance between the physical and the spiritual is restored to his life. 'Abdu'l-Baha states that through prayer a person enlarges his spiritual capacities. It is natural for human beings to pray to God for assistance and forgiveness and there are many prayers for all purposes in the Baha'i scriptures, but the highest prayer is the one that seeks nearness to God.

> I bear witness, O my God, that Thou hast created me to know Thee and to worship Thee. I testify, at this moment, to my powerlessness and to Thy might, to my poverty and to Thy wealth. There is none other God but Thee, the Help in Peril, the Self-Subsisting. (Short obligatory prayer revealed by Baha'u'llah, to be recited once in 24 hours, between noon and sunset.)

One aspect of the injunction to strive to know God through prayer and other spiritual practices is the fact that it reminds people of the purpose of their lives, provides them with guidance and direction, grounds them and gives them a sense of where they are in relation to the whole of creation. It enables them to know themselves better: 'Whatever duty Thou hast prescribed unto Thy servants of extolling to the utmost Thy majesty and glory is but a token of Thy grace unto them, that they may be enabled to ascend unto the station conferred upon their own inmost being, the station of the knowledge of their own selves' (Bahá'u'lláh, 1983, pp. 4–5).

It is also a Baha'i duty to read the scriptures each morning and evening. The Baha'i Faith has no clergy and thus reading the scriptures is one of the many ways of obtaining spiritual guidance from the highest source of this guidance that is available to human beings, the word of God. This reading, Baha'u'llah says, should not be excessive such that it causes fatigue but rather should be reflective and followed by meditation upon what has been read. According to the Baha'i teachings:

> It is an axiomatic fact that while you meditate you are speaking with your own spirit. In that state of mind you put certain questions to your spirit and the spirit answers: the light breaks

forth and the reality is revealed . . . The spirit of man is itself informed and strengthened during meditation; through it affairs of which man knew nothing are unfolded before his view. Through it he receives Divine inspiration, through it he receives heavenly food. *('Abdu'l-Bahá, 1967, p. 174)*

Indeed Baha'u'llah says that through this process, spiritual truth is revealed: 'Meditate profoundly, that the secret of things unseen may be revealed unto you, that you may inhale the sweetness of a spiritual and imperishable fragrance' (Bahá'u'lláh, 1989, p. 8).

The fasting period . . . is essentially a period of meditation and prayer, of spiritual recuperation, during which the believer must strive to make the necessary readjustments in his inner life, and to refresh and reinvigorate the spiritual forces latent in his soul. Its significance and purpose are, therefore, fundamentally spiritual in character. Fasting is symbolic, and a reminder of abstinence from selfish and carnal desires. (Shoghi Effendi, quoted in Baha'u'llah, 1992, pp. 176–7)

Another Baha'i practice that plays a key role in developing spirituality is fasting. Baha'is abstain from food and drink from sunrise to sunset for 19 days a year (those under 15, over 70, ill, pregnant or travelling are exempt from this). There are various statements in the Baha'i scriptures regarding the purpose and results of fasting: purification, self-discipline, coming to understand the sufferings of the poor of the world and the control of self and passion.

Baha'is also try, if they are able, to go on pilgrimage at least once in their lifetime to the shrines of the Baha'i Faith in the Haifa-'Akka area. Through visiting the shrines and the buildings associated with the lives of Baha'u'llah and the other central figures of the Baha'i Faith, Baha'is achieve a sense of closeness to them. Thus, the pilgrims return home spiritually renewed and reinvigorated.

Baha'u'llah states that the purpose of these laws is not some arbitrary exercise of power on the part of God, but rather they serve to guide and assist human beings in what will best help them to develop their spiritual reality. The more human beings practise these spiritual disciplines, the more they acquire spiritual attributes. The more they acquire these spiritual attributes, the more they draw near to and love God. Ultimately, according to the Baha'i scriptures, they should obey these laws, not for any hope of reward or fear of punishment, but out of love for God.

As individuals participate in the spiritual practices that Baha'u'llah has given, they become more able to use the opportunities that life presents to develop their spiritual qualities. Through these spiritual practices, they will read prayers beseeching God to help them to develop spiritual qualities such as love, patience, justice and forgiveness; they will read and meditate upon passages in the Baha'i scriptures about these qualities; and they will find in their daily life numerous opportunities to practise and perfect them. A person's daily life must, however, be consistent with her spiritual life. Prayers, fasting and meditation are meaningless if they do not result in spiritual development and spiritual development must show itself in a person's day-to-day life. A main purpose of the Baha'i Faith, indeed of the coming of Baha'u'llah, is to revolutionise society, to take it from its present level to a higher one: one that is more equitable and based on justice and love, and in which virtues such as honesty and trust-worthiness underpin government and drive social activity. For such a society to emerge, individuals who are spiritually transformed and who manifest these qualities must also emerge.

Many faiths teach that as life on earth is ephemeral there is little point in trying to improve it or even interact with it; rather, people must fix their gaze on the next world and try to be accepted there. Some people believe they must remove themselves from society and spend their time solely in contemplation and prayer. For some faiths, the devotional life requires the seclusion of the devotee and his separation from the day-to-day life of the world. Baha'u'llah prohibits such a lifestyle,[2] instead encouraging detachment from 'this world and the vanities thereof' (Bahá'u'lláh, 1983, p. 276), a subtle but important difference. Baha'is live the devotional life but they live it in the world, earning a livelihood through their work, which is elevated to the level of worship,[3] and engaging with others to create a society of justice, unity and peace in which all people can prosper. Baha'u'llah teaches that this physical world is a vital part of the human being's spiritual development. Indeed, it was created specifically for this purpose:

> Out of the wastes of nothingness, with the clay of My command I made thee to appear, and have ordained for thy training every atom in existence and the essence of all created things ... Out of My loving-kindness, 'neath the shade of My mercy I nurtured thee, and guarded thee by the essence of My grace and favour. And My purpose in all this was that thou mightest attain My everlasting dominion and become worthy of My invisible bestowals. *(Bahá'u'lláh, 1990, Persian 29)*

Therefore, a person's involvement with his family, his community and his world is an important part of his spiritual development.

Prayer and meditation are very important factors in deepening the spiritual life of the individual, but with them must go also action and example, as these are the tangible result of the former. Both are essential. (Shoghi Effendi, 1944)

Tests and Difficulties

In the course of one's spiritual journey on this earth, a person will undoubtedly come across tests and difficulties. Baha'u'llah explains that this is an inevitable part of progress. If one is turned towards the material world then these tests can become overwhelming and crippling. If, instead, one's values are turned towards the spiritual world, these tests can be viewed in a different light for it is by facing and overcoming these tests and by detaching oneself that a person develops spiritually. The pain experienced on the spiritual path is mostly caused by an attachment to the things of the physical world. It is painful to detach oneself from these. It is even more painful to detach oneself from what Baha'u'llah calls idle fancies and vain imaginings. Tests and difficulties also serve to prove a person's sincerity, to help him develop spiritual qualities such as patience and steadfastness, to teach him not to depend on the things of this world but upon God alone. Ultimately, they help the individual to pierce through the veils of the physical world and to discern the spiritual world more clearly. By struggling with tests and difficulties a person transcends them and reaches a higher plane in his spiritual progress.

Men who suffer not, attain no perfection. The plant most pruned by the gardeners is that one which, when the summer comes, will have the most beautiful blossoms and the most abundant fruit. The labourer cuts up the earth with his plough, and from that earth comes the rich and plentiful harvest. The more a man is chastened, the greater is the har- vest of spiritual virtues shown forth by him. ('Abdu'l-Bahá, 1967, p. 51)

This process of spiritual development requires sacrifice: the sacrifice of one's worldly attachments; the sacrifice of one's fond notions and vain fantasies; learning to sacrifice one's will to the will of God; sacrificing one's wealth voluntarily to help those less fortunate; sacrificing, if necessary, one's position in society, and perhaps even one's life, in order to stand up for one's beliefs. A major change in behaviour that promotes spiritual development is the sacrifice involved in being of service to others, service that assists those who are in need, service that teaches and educates others, and service that promotes the unity and peace of the world. Many in today's world have become obsessed with searching for their true selves. The Baha'i writings explain that 'The more we search for ourselves, the less likely we are to find ourselves; and the more we search for God, and to serve our fellow-men, the more profoundly will we become acquainted with ourselves, and the more inwardly assured. This is one of the great spiritual laws of life' (Shoghi Effendi, 1954). The Baha'i teachings state that even a person's daily work, carrying out a craft or trade or the like, should be carried out in the spirit of service and then it becomes worship.

Some people find the stress and anxiety generated by the modern world take over their lives while others become immersed in depression. The Baha'i teachings state that such problems have a spiritual aspect to them. They are generated by a value system that places the highest value on the things of this world – and people are never satisfied with what they have of those things. Whatever one has, one is always envious of the person who has more, bigger, better, newer things. But if this attitude changes so that the things of the spiritual world become most important, then even the poorest person can be rich in love, in patience, in justice and other spiritual values. And the more these spiritual qualities are reflected in the individual's behaviour, the more that person's life becomes pervaded by a deep sense of joy and contentment that is not disrupted by life's storms and tribulations. This personal spiritual transformation must, of course, manifest itself in the individual's social interactions. If it does not, it is probably delusory. This is why Baha'u'llah says, 'Let deeds, not words, be your adorning'. If one's spiritual development is reflected in one's interactions with others, then this will eventually have a transforming effect on society. And so the connection is made between the individual's life and society.

> . . . all the sorrow and the grief that exist come from the world of matter – the spiritual world bestows only the joy! . . . If we suffer it is the outcome of material things, and all the trials and troubles come from this world of illusion. For instance, a merchant may lose his trade and depression ensues. A work-man is dismissed and starvation stares him in the face. A farmer has a bad harvest, anxiety fills his mind . . . All these examples are to show you that the trials which beset our every step, all our sorrow, pain, shame and grief, are born in the world of matter; whereas the spiritual Kingdom never causes sadness. A man living with his thoughts in this Kingdom knows perpetual joy. The ills all flesh is heir to do not pass him by, but they only touch the surface of his life, the depths are calm and serene.

Today, humanity is bowed down with trouble, sorrow and grief, no one escapes; the world is wet with tears; but, thank God, the remedy is at our doors. Let us turn our hearts away from the world of matter and live in the spiritual world! It alone can give us freedom! If we are hemmed in by difficulties we have only to call upon God, and by His great Mercy we shall be helped.

If sorrow and adversity visit us, let us turn our faces to the Kingdom and heavenly consolation will be outpoured. If we are sick and in distress let us implore God's healing, and He will answer our prayer. When our thoughts are filled with the bitterness of this world, let us turn our eyes to the sweetness of God's compassion and He will send us heavenly calm! If we are imprisoned in the material world, our spirit can soar into the Heavens and we shall be free indeed!

When our days are drawing to a close let us think of the eternal worlds, and we shall be full of joy!' (*'Abdu'l-Bahá, 1967, pp. 110–11*)

Life after Death

The Baha'i Faith teaches that human beings are already an eternal spiritual reality, therefore their progress after the death of the physical body is a natural and inevitable event – it is merely the start of an eternal journey. However, progress can be more rapid if in this world they have 'packed the spiritual luggage' they need. This spiritual luggage consists of spiritual characteristics and virtues such as trustworthiness, generosity, kindness and patience. The development of these virtues is seen by Baha'is to be a fundamental purpose of one's life on earth. The goal of human life in this physical world must be to end life in a state that is as spiritually developed as possible. The reason for this is that after death, according to the Baha'i teachings, the person passes on to another life that is purely spiritual. Therefore, none of the material goods a person has accumulated nor his fame or social position will help him in that world. Only the extent to which he has developed himself spiritually in this world will help him in the next.

Very little can be known about the life that human beings have after death. All our vocabulary and knowledge are linked to experiences in this world. When a person dies he leaves behind this physical world and enters a spiritual one that is not limited by space or time. People therefore have no conceptual resources with which to begin even to imagine it. According to an analogy found in the Baha'i

In the beginning of his human life man was embryonic in the world of the matrix. There he received capacity and endowment for the reality of human existence. The forces and powers necessary for this world were bestowed upon him in that limited condition. In this world he needed eyes; he received them potentially in the other. He needed ears; he obtained them there in readiness and preparation for his new existence. The powers requisite in this world were conferred upon him in the world of the matrix so that when he entered this realm of real existence he not only possessed all necessary functions and powers but found provision for his material sustenance awaiting him.

Therefore, in this world he must prepare himself for the life beyond. That which he needs in the world of the Kingdom must be obtained here. Just as he prepared himself in the world of the matrix by acquiring forces necessary in this sphere of existence, so, likewise, the indispensable forces of the divine existence must be potentially attained in this world.

What is he in need of in the Kingdom which transcends the life and limitation of this mortal sphere? That world beyond is a world of sanctity and radiance; therefore, it is necessary that in this world he should acquire these divine attributes. In that world there is need of spirituality, faith, assurance, the knowledge and love of God. These he must attain in this world so that after his ascension from the earthly to the heavenly Kingdom he shall find all that is needful in that eternal life ready for him.

That divine world is manifestly a world of lights; therefore, man has need of illumination here. That is a world of love; the love of God is essential. It is a world of perfections; virtues, or perfections, must be acquired. That world is vivified by the breaths of the Holy Spirit; in this world we must seek them. That is the Kingdom of everlasting life; it must be attained during this vanishing existence.

By what means can man acquire these things? How shall he obtain these merciful gifts and powers? First, through the knowledge of God. Second, through the love of God. Third, through faith. Fourth, through philanthropic deeds. Fifth, through self-sacrifice. Sixth, through severance from this world. Seventh, through sanctity and holiness. Unless he acquires these forces and attains to these requirements, he will surely be deprived of the life that is eternal. ('Abdu'l-Bahá, 1982, pp. 225–6)

scriptures, it is no more possible to understand it than an embryo in the womb of its mother can understand this world. Baha'u'llah does, however, identify certain features (Bahá'u'lláh, 1983, pp. 155–7). For example, he indicates that the soul will continue to progress until it reaches the presence of God and will survive as long as God Himself exists. Realising that the significance of one's life lies as a preliminary to an eternal spiritual life changes one's viewpoint about what is important and what is not important in one's life. A person starts to orient his life towards this long-term vision. He changes his behaviour to take account of this.

In light of these teachings, it can be seen that the Baha'i view of salvation is somewhat different to that of other religions. One of the main transformations in understanding that the Baha'i teachings bring about is that they dispense with the idea that salvation is a state – in other words, that a person is either saved and is heading for heaven or is not saved and is condemned to hell. Rather, in the Baha'i Faith salvation is seen as a process or a journey. All individuals are at some point on this journey. Some are further ahead and some are behind. Some are travelling rapidly and some are almost immobile. The names hell and heaven are therefore merely relative terms. Those far ahead on the path are in heaven relative to those behind. Those who are moving slowly are in hell compared to those who are advancing rapidly. What the teachings of the founders of the world's religions do is to help people move more rapidly along this path. Furthermore, no one is really able to judge how far another person is along the path nor how fast they are travelling (it is difficult enough for an individual to achieve a state where she truly knows this about herself). Therefore, individuals are not to judge others or feel themselves to be in any way superior.

The part of the individual that goes on to life after death is called the soul, but since it is a spiritual reality little can be known about it. Baha'u'llah writes:

> Thou hast asked Me concerning the nature of the soul. Know, verily, that the soul is a sign of God, a heavenly gem whose reality the most learned of men hath failed to grasp, and whose mystery no mind, however acute, can ever hope to unravel. It is the first among all created things to declare the excellence of its Creator, the first to recognize His glory, to cleave to His truth, and to bow down in adoration before Him. If it be faithful to God, it will reflect His light, and will, eventually, return unto Him. If it fail, however, in its allegiance to its Creator, it will become a victim to self and passion, and will, in the end, sink in their depths. (Bahá'u'lláh, 1983, pp. 158–9)

> And now concerning thy question regarding the soul of man and its survival after death. Know thou of a truth that the soul, after its separation from the body, will continue to progress until it attaineth the presence of God, in a state and condition which neither the revolution of ages and centuries, nor the changes and chances of this world, can alter. It will endure as long as the Kingdom of God, His sovereignty, His dominion and power will endure. It will manifest the signs of God and His attributes, and will reveal His loving-kindness and bounty. The movement of My Pen is stilled when it attempteth to befittingly describe the loftiness and glory of so exalted a station. The honour with which the Hand of Mercy will invest the soul is such as no tongue can adequately reveal, nor any other earthly agency describe. Blessed is the soul which, at the hour of its separation from the body, is sanctified from the vain imaginings of the peoples of the world. Such a soul liveth and moveth in accordance with the Will of its Creator, and entereth the all-highest Paradise. (Bahá'u'-lláh, 1983, pp. 155–6)

The Spiritual Life and the Baha'i Community

The assistance that Baha'u'llah provides so that people may develop spiritually is not limited, however, to prayers and teachings. The entire structure of the Baha'i community is also focused on the twin objectives mentioned above: the refinement and growth of the individual's personal, inner, spiritual self, and the transformation of the social, collective life of humanity. Even the beauty of the Baha'i houses of worship is intended to uplift the spirit. Since the Baha'i Faith does not have priests, imams, gurus or other religious leaders to act as guides on the spiritual path, the structure and functioning of the Baha'i community itself acts in place of these.

Baha'u'llah states that whatever beneficial role religious leaders may have played in the past, they have also been a cause of the rejection of the Manifestations of God whenever each has come to the world. Now that humanity has the potential to educate everyone on the planet so that they can read the scriptures for themselves, there is no longer any need for this institution. Instead Baha'u'llah created a Baha'i administrative structure that has no individuals in positions of personal leadership or authority. Baha'u'llah also criticises those who blindly follow or imitate their religious leaders or guides. To do so leads to spiritual stagnation in that each generation merely continues the insights and guidance that it has inherited and does not push forward the boundaries of human spiritual achievement. Instead

Baha'u'llah wants all to investigate reality for themselves. He calls upon his followers to 'Tear asunder, in My Name, the veils that have grievously blinded your vision, and, through the power born of your belief in the unity of God, scatter the idols of vain imitation' (Bahá'u'lláh, 1983, p. 143).

Since, as seen above, everyone is now enjoined to follow the mystic path of spiritual development, the Baha'i administrative order becomes not just the administration of a religion but also the leadership of a mystic community and it fulfils the functions previously fulfilled by mystic communities, such as monasteries, and by spiritual guides, such as gurus and Sufi shaykhs. As mentioned above, part of the spiritual guidance needed can be obtained by prayer, study of the scriptures and meditation. However, the Baha'i teachings also make provision for tapping into the collective wisdom of the Baha'i community as a source of guidance. The process of consultation, which is applied in all aspects of Baha'i life, is also applied to the process of obtaining guidance from the scriptures. Groups of Baha'is come together and consult upon the meaning of passages of scripture, each putting forward their views freely and frankly and then discussing these in a loving and prayerful atmosphere. If the consultative process is working well, the end result transcends the ideas of the individual participants. Baha'u'llah calls consultation 'the lamp of guidance which leadeth the way and the bestower of true understanding' (Bahá'u'lláh, 1988b, p. 168), and 'Abdu'l-Baha states that 'the views of several individuals are assuredly preferable to one man, even as the power of a number of men is of course greater than the power of one man' (Bahá'u'lláh, cited in *Compilation* 1, 1991, pp. 97–8).

As well as providing spiritual guidance, the process of consultation can itself help the individual's spiritual progress. The qualities that are needed in the individual for good Baha'i consultation to occur are, according to the Baha'i scriptures: 'purity of motive, radiance of spirit, detachment from all else save God, attraction to His Divine Fragrances, humility and lowliness amongst His loved ones, patience and long-suffering in difficulties and servitude to His exalted Threshold' ('Abdu'l-Bahá, 1978, p. 87) – the very spiritual qualities that human beings are trying to develop. Thus, the more one participates thoughtfully and diligently in the consultative process, which occurs in all aspects of Baha'i community life, the more one progresses spiritually.

The central figures of the Baha'i Faith have always encouraged as much diversity in the Baha'i community as possible. Baha'is have been encouraged to enrol people of every race, ethnic group, religious background and social class into the Baha'i community. Consequently, as opposed to monastic communities where most individuals are from a similar background, many Baha'i communities are very diverse and each Baha'i is exposed to fellow-believers from social and cultural backgrounds which differ from their own. This results in numerous situations in which tests and conflicts can arise owing to a clash of opinions or of cultures. Commonly Baha'is report that their greatest tests come from their fellow-believers.

The tests and difficulties that arise are then resolved within the Baha'i community and there are several aspects of Baha'i community life that assist in this. Most community activity, even its administration, is carried out in an atmosphere of prayer and devotion; the members of the community are actively encouraged to interact with each other in an atmosphere of love and unity; and there is a prohibition on backbiting which, as Baha'u'llah says, 'quencheth the light of the heart, and extinguisheth the life of the soul' (Bahá'u'lláh, 1983, p. 265). The institution of the covenant ensures that, despite the natural tendency for this disparate group of individuals to break apart, the community remains united in its quest for a solution to the problems that arise. In brief, Baha'is try to create a religious community that is sufficiently supportive to allow the individuals in it to develop themselves spiritually within a 'safe' environment as a replacement for the monastic environment. As indicated above, it is precisely through overcoming these tests and difficulties that spiritual development occurs (and it is also, of course, through transcending these differences of culture and race that world unity can be built up at the local level).

The process of consultation and these community interactions also act as a corrective for any false ideas that an individual may have about how far he or she has progressed spiritually. It is easy to think that one is loving and patient when one is surrounded by other people from the same background as oneself in a monastic environment. It is much more difficult to be self-deluded about one's level of love and patience when one is interacting with individuals from widely differing backgrounds to one's own. Concomitant with Baha'u'llah's prohibition on the formation of monastic communities in the Baha'i Faith, he also encourages his followers to participate fully in the world. 'Be anxiously concerned with the needs of the age ye live in,' he writes, 'and centre your deliberations on its exigencies and requirements' (Bahá'u'lláh, 1983, p. 213). Thus Baha'is are encouraged to participate in social development projects and community activities wherever they live.

This participation in social processes is an aspect of the Baha'i teaching on the importance of service to humanity. There is a reciprocal relationship between one's level of service and one's spiritual progress. The more one serves, the more one advances spiritually; the more one advances spiritually, the more opportunities for service present themselves. There is also a reciprocal relationship in the development of spiritual qualities through participating in social activities in a spirit of service. One needs to have developed spiritual qualities in order to participate effectively and constructively, but, also, participation assists the individual to acquire or perfect these qualities. One comes to value and therefore to acquire trustworthiness if one participates in any situation where community leadership is called for; one comes to value and acquire justice when one participates in activities designed to improve the rights of minorities in society or works to ameliorate global poverty; one comes to learn patience if one begins to deal with the disadvantaged in society. This leads to the concept that what Baha'is are working for is not so much individual salvation but a collective, social salvation. In other words, an individual's thoughts and actions should be concentrated on what will be of service to others and will promote the general good (and here the general good means that of the whole world and not just one's own corner of it) and by doing this individuals will best benefit their own individual spiritual development and salvation. Therefore, personal salvation is bound up in an interconnected and interdependent way with the salvation of the world.

2

Personal Life

The individual human being is unique in creation. Baha'is believe that the human individual is essentially spiritual in nature. While the body is alive, the physical, emotional and intellectual capacities of the individual are integrated with the life of the soul. The purpose of life is the spiritual advancement of the soul by drawing nearer to God and worshipping Him.

Thus the Baha'i Faith, like all religions, addresses the spiritual life of the individual. Baha'is believe that the soul comes into being at the time of the conception of the body and continues to be associated with it throughout the physical life of the body. While the soul of the human being is immortal, the body eventually grows old and dies and the two separate, the body decaying and returning to the earth and the soul continuing its eternal journey.

Health

While the body is alive, the soul and the body are intimately connected and have an effect on each other. It is the purpose of the body to serve as a vehicle for the soul while it is on the earth and as such the day-to-day life, practices and habits of the body are significant insofar as they assist the soul in its development. Thus while Baha'is focus on their spiritual life, they are also alert to the need to care for their body, to keep it healthy and not to endanger, harm or pollute it. Further, many physical practices and exercises are outward manifestations of spiritual realities or symbols of a spiritual condition. Thus, for example, the physical abstinence from food during the Baha'i fast is both a spiritual exercise designed to assist the development of spiritual qualities and an outward symbol of a spiritual state of being.

As one of the purposes of religion is to establish unity at all levels, Baha'is believe that human beings must manifest this unity themselves, that is, all facets of the self – the spiritual, physical, emotional and intellectual – should be integrated and the well-being of none of them neglected or compromised. Further, all aspects and activities of one's daily life are informed by one's spiritual health and can, at the same time, have an effect on one's spirit. Thus those things which tend to interfere with the proper functioning of the body or the mind, such as alcohol and drugs, are prohibited by the Baha'i teachings and those things which tend to keep the body healthy, such as cleanliness, uplift the spirit, such as music, or stimulate the mind, such as scientific enquiry, are encouraged.

Baha'is consider the body to be the 'temple of the spirit' (Shoghi Effendi, 1957a) and therefore it is to be treated with honour. It should be kept healthy, not only out of respect but because it is the body that enables a person to serve others and because the unity of the self must be preserved for the human being to function spiritually. Many of the teachings of Baha'u'llah with regard to the care of the body are directed to this end.

A number of the teachings of Baha'u'llah centre around the cleanliness of the body, one's clothes and one's home. Baha'is are exhorted to be 'the very essence of cleanliness amongst mankind' (Bahá'u'lláh, 1992, para. 74), to adopt practices that are 'most in keeping with refinement' (ibid. para. 46) and to be graceful. The Arabic word *litafat*, often translated as 'refinement' or 'cleanliness' in the Baha'i writings, has 'a wide range of meanings with both spiritual and physical implications, such as elegance, gracefulness, cleanliness, civility, politeness, gentleness, delicacy and graciousness, as well as being subtle, refined, sanctified and pure' (Universal House of Justice, quoted in ibid. note 74, p. 199). Hence Baha'u'llah stipulates that a person should wash his whole body at least weekly in fresh, clean water, wash his feet every day in summer and at least every three days in winter, wash his clothes, pare his nails and cut his hair, although not shave it. Baha'is are not to eat with their hands from a communal bowl. These provisions ensured the health of the Baha'i community at a time when little was known about the spread of disease and when plumbing was primitive. So important are cleanliness and pure habits that 'Abdu'l-Baha wrote a prayer on the subject, beseeching God to keep Baha'is free 'from all defilement, and released from all addictions', to 'save them from committing any repugnant act' and to

---

First in a human being's way of life must be purity, then freshness, cleanliness, and independence of spirit . . . in every aspect of life, purity and holiness, cleanliness and refinement, exalt the human condition and further the development of man's inner reality. Even in the physical realm, cleanliness will conduce to spirituality, as the Holy Writings clearly state. And although bodily cleanliness is a physical thing, it hath, nevertheless, a powerful influence on the life of the spirit.' ('Abdu'l-Bahá, 1978, pp. 146–7)

release them from the 'chains of every evil habit' ('Abdu'l-Bahá, 1978, p. 149). Baha'is are to keep their homes clean and tidy and to renew their home furnishings after 19 years, if they can afford to do so. Parents should also ensure their children are clean, well mannered and well behaved. Schoolchildren should be dressed in clean clothes and their schools should be kept clean and located, if possible, where the air is pure.

Baha'is recognise that good health is more than the absence of disease and encompasses physical, mental, emotional, intellectual and spiritual well-being, each having an impact on the other. The health of the body is to be maintained through diet, rest and exercise and by following the advice of competent physicians. 'Abdu'l-Baha indicated that a mother's milk is best for an infant, if she is at all able to feed it herself ('Abdu'l-Bahá, in *Compilation*, 1991, vol. 1, p. 461). He pointed out that human teeth are not designed for tearing meat but for grinding grain, cutting fruit and cracking nuts and stated that 'it would undoubtedly be better and more pleasing' if people would content themselves with 'cereals, fruit, oil and nuts, such as pistachios, almonds and so on' (ibid. p. 462). He predicted that in the future people will be vegetarians but stated that Baha'is are not forbidden to eat meat, including pork, remarking that 'Meat is nourishing and containeth the elements of herbs, seeds and fruits; therefore sometimes it is essential for the sick and for the rehabilitation of health. There is no objection in the Law of God to the eating of meat if it is required. So if thy constitution is rather weak and thou findest meat useful, thou mayest eat it' (ibid. p. 463). Baha'is are advised not to overindulge but to eat moderately, having a single course of good quality food if one can afford it (Bahá'u'lláh, in ibid. p. 459). They are advised that they should not eat unless they are hungry. 'Abdu'l-Baha recommends walking a little after a meal but not exercising on a full stomach. In general, however, exercise is good for the muscles, he states.

Baha'is are encouraged to protect their health by getting enough sleep and relaxation (see, for example, Shoghi Effendi, 1952b), forcing themselves, if necessary, 'to take time, and not only for prayer and meditation, but for real rest and relaxation' (Shoghi Effendi, 1947). The purpose of sleep, however, is not merely to protect one's health but 'to rest the body in order to do better, to speak better, to explain more beautifully, to serve the servants of God and to prove the truths' ('Abdu'l-Bahá, in *Baha'i World Faith*, 1976, p. 384).

The Baha'i teachings on sexual health rest on the principle that sexual relations are to be confined to marriage partners. For the individual, this does not mean the 'suppression of the sex impulse but . . . its regulation and control' (Shoghi Effendi, 1938) through marriage.

From the perspective of personal health, the advantage of such safe sex is clear, as are the social implications for creating strong families, on the one hand, and preventing problems in society such as the spread of HIV/AIDS, on the other.

In the first instance, parents are responsible for safeguarding the health of their children, for ensuring that they are appropriately fed and protected from illness. The role of mothers is central. As they are usually the first and primary carers of children, the ones who are most aware when illness strikes their children or others in the family, they are particularly influential in maintaining the health of the family and in shaping the habits of a healthy lifestyle. To assist mothers in this role, the Baha'i teachings promote the education of women and, because women have such insights into primary health care, Baha'is urge governments to solicit the opinions of women when deciding public health policy and they advocate the inclusion of women on decision-making bodies.

In keeping with the emphasis Baha'is place on the importance of women and mothers, they strongly promote programmes that address the health of women, on whom so many families and communities depend. They advocate that particular effort should be made to ensure that women receive adequate nutrition, especially girls, who in many societies are the last members of a family to be fed. Baha'is believe girls and women need to be protected from harmful cultural practices and traditions such as genital mutilation, particularly in adolescence. As people are living longer, attention must also be turned to safeguarding the physical, mental and spiritual health of older women, particularly widows, who are among the most vulnerable in some societies.

Baha'is consider that it is important to ensure that the messages about health do not cast women as victims but rather treat them as participants in decisions about their own well-being. Baha'is have found the use of traditional, local media, such as folk music and folk theatre, to be effective ways to communicate difficult messages to target audiences. However, in advancing these ideas and projects, Baha'is are conscious that messages about women's health issues are often best directed not only to women themselves but to men, who in many societies control families, decision-making bodies, resources and government.

The Baha'i approach to healing is in keeping with Baha'u'llah's teaching on the harmony of science and religion: they believe that the best results can be obtained by combining both spiritual and physical processes.

Baha'u'llah charged Baha'is who become ill to seek medical advice from a competent physician – 'doctors who have studied a scientific system of medicine' (Shoghi Effendi, 1948) – and to follow the doctor's instructions ('Abdu'l-Bahá, 1978, p. 156). No specific school of medicine, healing or nutrition is associated with the Baha'i Faith and none are particularly promoted. Individuals are to decide themselves what doctors to consult but have an obligation 'to distinguish between doctors who are well trained in medical sciences and those who are not' (Universal House of Justice, 1977). Baha'is are encouraged to study medicine and to practise it, as it is considered to be a useful profession. At the same time, it is recognised that medicine is still in its infancy and thus imperfect. Baha'is are urged to develop the science of medicine to such a high degree that in the future they will be able to heal with 'foods, ailments, fragrant fruits and vegetables, and by various waters, hot and cold in temperature' ('Abdu'l-Bahá, 1981, p. 259). Baha'is may become organ donors if they wish.

There are no Baha'i 'healers' such as are found in, for example, Christian Science, although it is accepted that some people do have the ability to assist the healing of others (Shoghi Effendi, 1948). Baha'is acknowledge that it is possible to heal some sicknesses through spiritual means by turning to God in prayer and that 'physical healing cannot be complete and lasting unless it is reinforced by spiritual healing' (Shoghi Effendi, 1935b). The Baha'i approach is pragmatic: 'Disease is of two kinds: material and spiritual. Take for instance, a cut hand; if you pray for the cut to be healed and do not stop its bleeding, you will not do much good; a material remedy is needed. Sometimes if the nervous system is paralysed through fear, a spiritual remedy is necessary . . . It often happens that sorrow makes one ill, this can be cured by spiritual means' ('Abdu'l-Bahá quoted in 'Abdu'l-Bahá in London', p. 65). These two forms of healing are not considered contradictory and Baha'is should 'accept the physical remedies as coming from the mercy and favour of God', who 'revealed and made manifest medical science so that His servants may profit from this kind of treatment' ('Abdu'l-Bahá, in Bahá'í World Faith, 1976, p. 376). Baha'is are free to follow alternative therapies if they wish and 'to investigate new things, and use them if they prove of real value and no harm' (Shoghi Effendi, 1952a).

Regarding your questions concerning the condition of the soul during illness . . . physical ailments, no matter how severe, cannot bring any change in the inherent condition of the soul. As Bahá'u'lláh says: "The spirit is permanent and steadfast in its station." The veil or hindrance that interposes between soul and body during physical disease is sickness itself. (Shoghi Effendi, 1936b)

Baha'is consider mental illness to be a medical issue and not a spiritual disease or one that affects one's inner relationship to God. As with any debilitating illness, 'its effects may indeed hinder and be a burden in one's striving toward spiritual progress' (Universal House of Justice, 1982). Again, the assistance of physicians, including psychiatrists, should be sought.

The Baha'i teachings 'condemn, emphatically and unequivocally, any form of physical violence' (Shoghi Effendi, 1939b), including against oneself. Similarly, substances which injure the body, incapacitate it, render it unable to function properly or impair the essential unity of the self, such as alcohol and habit-forming drugs, are forbidden to Baha'is. 'Heroin, hashish and other derivatives of cannabis such as marijuana, as well as hallucinogenic agents such as LSD, peyote and similar substances, are regarded as falling under this prohibition' (Universal House of Justice, quoted in Baha'u'llah, 1992, note 170, p. 238). Particularly condemned is the use of opium which, in addition to having a deleterious effect on physical health, 'Abdu'l-Baha says 'fasteneth on the soul so that the user's conscience dieth, his mind is blotted away, his perceptions are eroded. It turneth the living into the dead. It quencheth the natural heat' ('Abdu'l-Bahá, 1978, p. 149). Baha'is are permitted to smoke tobacco, but it is described as 'dirty, smelly, offensive – an evil habit' that is 'repugnant from the standpoint of hygiene' and consequently 'the smoker is vulnerable to many and various diseases' (ibid. pp. 147–8).

Arts

In contrast are those things that have a positive and beneficial effect on both the body and the spirit. Physical health can be affected by the uplifting of the spirit that comes from a beautiful environment and the arts.

> It is natural for the heart and spirit to take pleasure and enjoyment in all things that show forth symmetry, harmony, and perfection. For instance: a beautiful house, a well designed garden, a symmetrical line, a graceful motion, a well written book, pleasing garments – in fact, all things that have in themselves grace or beauty are pleasing to the heart and spirit . . .
> *('Abdu'l-Bahá, quoted in Lucas, 1905, pp. 11–14)*

Baha'is recognise the beauty of nature and are encouraged to cultivate beauty in their homes and gardens and in the wider environment. For example, great attention is given to the beauty of the architecture, landscaping and setting of Baha'i shrines and buildings and Baha'is at the United Nations have advocated the promotion of beauty as a guiding principle in community planning (Bahá'í International Community, 1996a).

As for the arts, Baha'u'llah considered them so important in themselves that he raised them to the level of worship (see 'Abdu'l-Baha, 1967, p. 176 and *Baha'i World Faith*, 1976, p. 377). He described music as a ladder for the soul and one of the most important arts. Although it derives from the physical realm, being vibrations of the air, it has a tremendous spiritual effect, freeing the listener from care and sorrow ('Abdu'l-Bahá, 1978, p. 112), making the spirit happy or exciting it to action ('Abdu'l-Bahá quoted in Lucas, 1905, pp. 11–14). Baha'is are thus recommended to set their scriptures to beautiful music and to sing their prayers. Similarly, poetry can greatly influence the soul more effectively than prose: 'It stirs more deeply, for it is of a finer composition' (ibid.). Baha'i parents are encouraged to teach their child to sing and play music and to develop an appreciation for this and others arts.

Work

Baha'u'llah gave artists and craftsmen a high rank and stated that they 'should be appreciated, for they advance the affairs of mankind'. He emphasised that 'the means of livelihood depend upon those who are engaged in arts and crafts' (Bahá'u'lláh, in *Compilation*, 1991, vol. 1, p. 3). This focus on the contribution that artists and craftsmen make to society is in keeping with the general Baha'i approach to work. Baha'u'llah raised work done in the spirit of service to humanity to the rank of worship and exhorted everyone – even those with disabilities – to work. Although different professions, sciences, arts and crafts are mentioned in the Baha'i teachings as being useful to society, the sort of work undertaken is left up to individuals to determine. Homemaking and looking after children are considered honourable and responsible forms of work. Whatever work a Baha'i chooses to perform, he should strive for excellence, and in his work, whether as an employer or an employee, he should demonstrate his adherence to the high moral and ethical standard set by Baha'u'llah. Organisations such as the European Baha'i Business Forum have developed a set of core values based on the Baha'i teachings which employers and employees alike may find useful.

Begging as a way of life is prohibited in the Baha'i Faith. It is the responsibility of government to ensure that people are able to get the training and education they need to find employment and that they have the opportunity to use their skills. Not only does work provide individuals and families with a source of income, it also has a value in itself in that it draws people closer to God and helps them understand His purpose for them. Thus merely having wealth does not exempt people from daily work, nor do disabilities. Further, the Baha'i writings do not mention a retirement age. However, if a person is completely incapacitated, or falls into extreme poverty, then it becomes the responsibility of the state to provide him with a monthly allowance.

Wealth, Poverty and Voluntary Giving

The Baha'i attitude to work is indicative of their attitude to money and hence to wealth and poverty. One of the purposes of Baha'u'llah's advent was to eliminate the extremes of wealth and poverty. This does not mean Baha'is advocate that there should be absolute equality of wealth among individuals or families – this is impossible and undesirable and not conducive to the smooth running of society. Further, Baha'is recognise that people differ in their abilities and skills, and that they will therefore do different work; consequently, they should receive an income that reflects these differences. Baha'u'llah therefore advocates the voluntary sharing of wealth, whether by wealthy individuals to those less well off or by wealthy states to poorer ones.

To facilitate such giving and to avoid the negative connotations of donors and recipients, Baha'u'llah instituted the 'Right of God' (Huququ'llah), whereby individual Baha'is offer 19 per cent of their capital gains to the head of the religion – today the Universal House of Justice – to be expended on specified categories of recipients: the poor, the disabled, the needy and orphans and the essential needs of the Baha'i Faith itself. This is not merely an economic exercise but a spiritual responsibility and privilege, the effects of which redound on the donor.

The freely made decision to share part of one's substance with others is a sign of the maturity of the individual and of humanity and a marker along the road to universal prosperity and, ultimately, peace. While it may seem odd to base an economic system on love, this is essentially the Baha'i position: recognition of the oneness of the human family and a cementing of hearts will inspire individuals, families, communities and ultimately nations to offer economic assistance to others in the same way that members of one family might help each other. At a personal level, the giving of charity is considered a meritorious deed. Baha'is believe there is no shame in being poor – just as there is no merit in being rich – and that those with greater wealth should have the 'utmost regard' for those who have less (Bahá'u'lláh, 1983, p. 202).

Social Responsibility and Service to Others

This sense of social responsibility towards others is a distinguishing feature of a Baha'i's personal life. It is bound up with the teaching about service to humanity, which is a driving principle for Baha'is, and is linked to Baha'u'llah's admonition that people should not live as hermits, secluded monks or aesthetes. Because Baha'u'llah gives service to others a high station and likens it to service to God, a Baha'i would naturally become involved in the activities and programmes of his or her local and national community and is likely to volunteer his or her services freely for the betterment of the community. Thus, for example, in trying to put into practice Baha'u'llah's statement that to educate someone else's child is like bringing up one of his (Bahá'u'lláh, 1988b, p. 128), a Baha'i might decide to foster a child. Similarly, Baha'is and their communities are engaged in a wide variety of sustainable social and economic development projects at the grassroots level that are maintained by local Baha'is, so an individual Baha'i may find herself working on such a project. Or if the Baha'is do not have such a project themselves, a Baha'i is likely to volunteer to work at a project or activity sponsored by another group.

Such social involvement is linked to the principle that one should continually search for truth and educate oneself. Baha'is are to keep themselves informed of what is going on in the world around them and to try to correlate the teachings of Baha'u'llah with those events, to offer what is needed and relevant, not just 'do good'. Keeping oneself abreast of current affairs and how the Baha'i Faith might touch on them requires constant education of oneself and relies on a belief in one's capacity to search for truth and to benefit from the result: a recognition of the fact that human consciousness is endowed with the intellectual, moral, spiritual, and aesthetic capacities needed to undertake such an effort. (Bahá'í International Community, 1993).

Participation in and engagement with the everyday issues affecting the lives and welfare of people are an aspect of the spiritual life of every Baha'i. 'Be anxiously concerned', Baha'u'llah says, 'with the needs of the age ye live in, and centre your deliberations on its exigencies and requirements' (Bahá'u'lláh, 1983, p. 213). However, Baha'is do not involve themselves in partisan politics as a way of achieving this because they are divisive and would negate the very unity that is the

> Be ye loving fathers to the orphan, and a refuge to the helpless, and a treasury for the poor, and a cure for the ailing. Be ye the helpers of every victim of oppression, the patrons of the disadvantaged. Think ye at all times of rendering some service to every member of the human race. Pay ye no heed to aversion and rejection, to disdain, hostility, injustice: act ye in the opposite way. Be ye sincerely kind, not in appearance only. Let each one of God's loved ones centre his attention on this: to be the Lord's mercy to man; to be the Lord's grace. Let him do some good to every person whose path he crosseth, and be of some benefit to him. Let him improve the character of each and all, and reorient the minds of men. In this way, the light of divine guidance will shine forth, and the blessings of God will cradle all mankind: for love is light, no matter in what abode it dwelleth; and hate is darkness, no matter where it may make its nest. ('Abdu'l-Bahá, 1978, p. 3)

main goal of the Baha'i Faith. They neither run for office nor canvas for political parties or individual politicians. They may vote in elections, if it is possible to do so without identifying themselves with a particular political party, and they may serve in government positions so long as these are not identified as party political.

At the same time, Baha'is believe that the universal application of the Baha'i teachings to social problems is the most effective way to resolve them and that they also need to build up the Baha'i system so that it can serve as a model of how to do this. To this end a Baha'i will generally be an active participant in the activities, programmes and plans of his or her local Baha'i community and involved in its promulgation and administration. Many Baha'is offer their own homes for these activities. Similarly, the offering of hospitality is characteristic of Baha'is and their homes are often open to friends and strangers as a way of showing genuine friendship and furthering the Baha'i principles.

Balanced Living and Relationships

Having such high aspirations for themselves and such an active agenda, it might be assumed that Baha'is have no time left over for themselves or their families. Yet Baha'is strive to live a balanced life in which the development and growth of every aspect of the individual – spiritual, intellectual, emotional and physical – is nurtured and finds a higher expression through one's family, work, social activities, community involvement, recreation and Baha'i activities. For Baha'is, the building up of relationships between marriage partners, family members, friends and the wider community and giving adequate amounts of time to sustain them are vital to the overall health not only of the individual but of the planet, as it is these relationships that create the unity that must be the foundation of all human endeavour. At the same time, having sufficient time for personal reflection and education, rest and recreation are also important and every individual must decide how best to combine all these into his or her own life so that he or she does not become stressed or overly exhausted.

Living a balanced life also implies living a life of moderation. Baha'u'llah enjoined 'moderation in all things' (ibid. p. 216.), and while leaving individuals free to choose their own life styles, dress and behaviours, he expected them to understand that this was within the context of the standards of chastity and holiness which underpin the spiritualised life. Thus 'the exercise of moderation in all that pertains to dress, language, amusements, and all artistic and literary avocations' is for the Baha'i coupled with the 'abandonment of a frivolous conduct, with its excessive attachment to trivial and often misdirected pleasures', 'total abstinence from all alcoholic drinks' and 'habit-forming drugs' and faithfulness to one's marriage partner (Shoghi Effendi, 1990, p. 30). Baha'is see that in the world today there is 'an almost frenetic devotion to pleasure and diversion, an insatiable thirst for amusement, a fanatical devotion to games and sport, a reluctance to treat any matter seriously, and a scornful, derisory attitude towards virtue and solid worth' (Universal House of Justice, 1979).

At the same time, 'the maintenance of such a high standard of moral conduct is not to be associated or confused with any form of asceticism, or of excessive and bigoted puritanism. The standard inculcated by Baha'u'llah does not seek, under any circumstances, to deny anyone the legitimate right and privilege to derive the fullest advantage and benefit from the manifold joys, beauties, and pleasures with which the world has been so plentifully enriched by an All-Loving Creator' (Shoghi Effendi, 1990, p. 33). 'Humour, happiness, joy are characteristics of a true Baha'i life. Frivolity palls and eventually leads to boredom and emptiness, but true happiness and joy and humour that are parts of a balanced life that includes serious thought, compassion and humble servitude to God, are characteristics that enrich life and add to its radiance' (Universal House of Justice, 1979). Thus Baha'is are not perpetually solemn, nor are they prohibited from enjoying even the trivial pleasures of life. The balance the individual seeks is the path of moderation between excessive attachment to such pleasures and the excessive piety that leads to asceticism.

The Search for Truth

The human spirit must be free to know. Apprehending who we are, for what purpose we exist, and how we should live our lives, is a basic impulse of human consciousness. This quest for self-understanding and meaning is the essence of life itself. The innate and fundamental aspiration to investigate reality is thus a right and an obligation of every human being. It is for this reason that the Baha'i teachings affirm that the 'conscience of man is sacred and to be respected'.

To search for truth – to see with one's 'own eyes and not through the eyes of others' – is to undertake a process of spiritual discovery with a keen sense of justice and openness. It is by its very nature a process that is creative and transformative; if pursued with sincerity and fairness, it can bestow upon the seeker of knowledge 'a new eye, a new ear, a new heart, and a new mind'. The rational soul is thereby awakened to the capacities of kindness, forbearance, and compassion that lie within it. Clearly, the human yearning for truth is a power that cannot be shackled, for without the freedom to know, human nature remains the prisoner of instinct, ignorance and desire. *(Bahá'í International Community, 2001b)*

Development of the Intellect: Education

'Abdu'l-Baha indicated that 'God's greatest gift to man is that of intellect', noting that of all creation, it is only human beings who have this faculty ('Abdu'l-Bahá, 1967, p. 41). Baha'u'llah declared that 'Knowledge is as wings to man's life, and a ladder for his ascent. Its acquisition is incumbent upon everyone' (Baha'u'llah, 1988b, p. 51). Thus, just as the individual is to progress and mature spiritually, to take care of his or her body and to live moderately and morally, education, the development of the intellect and fostering an attitude of intellectual enquiry are indispensable to the development of the unified human being that is so essential to the establishment of a unified world society.

The Baha'i writings indicate that there are three sorts of education: material, which deals with the development of the body; human, which is the knowledge of arts and sciences; and spiritual, which is concerned with the development of character and the acquisition of values. Baha'is are to avail themselves of all three and to provide them for their children. They should concentrate on those sciences and arts that will benefit themselves and their families, advance human knowledge and further the interests of all humanity. Interestingly, according to Shoghi Effendi, one of the benefits that will accrue from the establishment of world peace will be that the financial resources now spent on war will be spent on the 'sharpening and refinement of the human brain' (Shoghi Effendi, 1991, p. 204).

Decision-making and Problem-solving

Every person is called upon to make decisions, whether important or insignificant, every day. Baha'is are encouraged to consult others before making decisions, particularly important decisions that affect one's life and the life of others. Consultation enables a person to see things in a different light, to gain new insights and to consider aspects of the situation he might not have appreciated. Similarly, Baha'is are to solve their problems – including personal and family problems and those that are work-related – through consultation. The purpose of consultation is the investigation of truth.

Suffering

While it is the natural right and aspiration of every human being to strive for and achieve personal happiness, Baha'is accept that every life is touched by suffering and that human nature is refined by it. The tests and trials of life can be beneficial, both to the individual, by assisting him to develop his spiritual qualities, and to society at large, by enabling it to reform those elements of life which cause suffering. This is not to imply that Baha'is are to inflict suffering on others or on themselves, are to stand by while others suffer or should not do every-thing in their power to prevent the widespread suffering we see today in the world. This is far from the case. One of the main purposes of the Baha'i religion is to prevent suffering, which Baha'is believe is the result of social injustice that comes from the world ignoring the teach-ings of Baha'u'llah. Hence, at the individual level, a most effective way to prevent suffering is to promote the Baha'i Faith and to put into practice the Baha'i spiritual and social teachings. In addition, individ-ual Baha'is are to visit the sick, show generosity to others, voluntarily share their wealth, give to charity and offer hospitality. To alleviate their own suffering, to overcome stress and to cope with change, they are to pray, bring themselves to account each day for their own deeds and meditate on the Baha'i writings, as well as make the modifications to their own life that may be required. 'Abdu'l-Baha indicated that children and vulnerable people who suffer in this world will be recompensed in the next and that the wisdom of this will eventually be known ('Abdu'l-Bahá, in *Baha'i World Faith*, 1976, p. 372).

> [Baha'u'llah] hath consented to be bound with chains that mankind may be released from its bondage, and hath accepted to be made a prisoner within this most mighty Stronghold that the whole world may attain unto true liberty. He hath drained to its dregs the cup of sorrow, that all the peoples of the earth may attain unto abiding joy, and be filled with gladness . . . We have accepted to be abased, O believers in the Unity of God, that ye may be exalted, and have suffered manifold afflictions, that ye might prosper and flourish. (Bahá'u'lláh, 1983, p. 99)

Death

At the end of the body's life, the soul separates from the body and continues in the next world as a spiritual entity. Baha'u'llah stated that God has made death 'a messenger of joy' (Baha'u'llah, 1990, Arabic 32) to the departed soul, a perspective wholly consistent with the Baha'i view of the afterlife.

The respect that is to be shown to the body while a person is alive is to be extended to it after its death. The Bab stated that after death the body should be 'preserved to the extent possible' (The Báb, 1976, p. 95) and the Baha'i teachings state that because the body housed the spirit while on earth, it must be treated with dignity. The laws surrounding the burial and funeral of a deceased Baha'i reflect the belief that the body was once the 'throne of the inner temple' (ibid.) and should therefore not be burned or merely discarded, even though Baha'u'llah confirmed that after death the spirit is no longer connected to the body. Thus Baha'is are to be buried in the ground, 'with radiance and serenity in a nearby place' (Bahá'u'lláh, 1992, para. 130) so that their bodies decompose naturally and gradually; they should not be cremated. The body is to be wrapped in five sheets of silk or cotton or, for those who have limited means, a single sheet. A burial-ring bearing the inscription 'I came forth from God, and return unto Him, detached from all save Him, holding fast to His Name, the Merciful, the Compassionate' (ibid. para. 128) is to be placed on the deceased's finger. Coffins should be made of 'crystal, of hard, resistant stone or of wood that is both fine and durable' (ibid.). These three provisions are not yet binding on non-Iranian Baha'is but are sometimes observed by them.

The body is not to be transported more than an hour's journey from the place of death, thus preventing the long 'caravans of death', so common in the days of Baha'u'llah, that carried decomposing corpses to the sacred shrines so that the faithful could be buried near Islamic holy men.

As the Baha'i Faith has no clergy, the funeral service for a deceased Baha'i is generally arranged by the local Baha'i institution, the local spiritual assembly, in consultation with the family and is often conducted by family members and friends. Before interment an obligatory prayer for the dead is recited by one person while all others present stand. Baha'is often include other prayers and readings from scripture, as well as music and poetry, at funeral services.

Being a Baha'i

The individual is the bedrock of the Baha'i Faith. Although the religion calls for greater and greater levels of unity, from the family to the whole planet, nevertheless, it is the individual Baha'i on which the whole structure relies. 'He it is who constitutes the warp and woof on which the quality and pattern of the whole fabric must depend. He it is who acts as one of the countless links in the mighty chain that now girdles the globe . . . Without his support, at once whole-hearted, continuous and generous, every measure adopted, and every plan formulated . . . is foredoomed to failure' (Shoghi Effendi, 1965, pp. 130–1). As the religion is without clergy, its functioning depends on the voluntary efforts of its individual members and its propagation, development and protection rest in the hands of ordinary believers. Baha'is accept that they have a huge responsibility to take their Faith forward – to teach others about it and to establish, finance and maintain its institutions; only registered Baha'is are allowed to contribute to the funds of the religion. Far from considering this a burden, Baha'is consider it a spiritual and sacred privilege to undertake the tasks of their Faith, recognising, in the words of Shoghi Effendi:

> Ours is then the duty and privilege to labour, by day and by night, amidst the storm and stress of these troublous days, that we may quicken the zeal of our fellow-men, rekindle their hopes, stimulate their interest, open their eyes to the true Faith of God and enlist their active support in the carrying out of our common task for the peace and regeneration of the world. (Shoghi Effendi, 1968, p. 51)

> A 'best teacher' and an 'exemplary believer' is ultimately neither more nor less than an ordinary Baha'i who has consecrated himself to the work of the Faith, deepened his knowledge and understanding of its Teachings, placed his confidence in Baha'u'llah, and arisen to serve Him to the best of his ability. (Shoghi Effendi, 1957b)

Being a Baha'i means aligning one's life with the principles of Baha'u'llah and living in accordance with the Baha'i teachings. Baha'u'llah teaches that the 'first duty' given by God to humanity is to recognise the divine teacher sent by God while the second is to obey his laws (Bahá'u'lláh, 1992, para. 1). Daily prayer, meditation and the reading of holy scripture and the annual fast are practices designed to assist the development of one's spiritual life. Baha'is make great efforts to rid themselves of prejudice, to become trustworthy, to shun violence and to develop their spiritual qualities. Participation in the activities and administration of the Baha'i community is an outward expression of one's devotion to the religion and assists in developing its strength and unity. Baha'is promote unity, harmony, fellowship, justice and peace in their families, communities, workplaces and in the world.

There are a number of customs and laws in other religions that are not part of the Baha'i Faith. These include the confession of sins, the kissing of hands, prostrating oneself before another human being, regarding human beings or things as impure, dietary prohibitions and rituals of initiation such as baptism. Baha'is are also discouraged from creating new rituals and customary practices.

Becoming a Baha'i

A Baha'i is someone who has recognized Baha'u'llah as the great teacher, or Manifestation of God, for this time and is willing to follow his teachings. The very act of recognising Baha'u'llah is what makes a person a Baha'i – there is no other action required. In some places Baha'i communities ask a person to sign a registration card or to write a letter so that they have a note of the person's contact details and can ensure that the person is entitled to contribute to the Baha'i funds and to vote in Baha'i elections. Many Baha'i communities regard the 'declaration' of a new Baha'i as a joyous occasion to be celebrated.

Children born into Baha'i families are brought up to understand the Baha'i teachings and principles and to love Baha'u'llah, but at around the age of 15 they must make their own decision about whether they will be Baha'is.

For those who come across the Baha'i Faith later in life, the decision to become a Baha'i, 'changing religion', is usually a momentous one and affects all aspects of a person's life and every relationship. Most Baha'is today are themselves converts and they therefore understand the challenges that becoming a Baha'i can entail. Hence, they make special efforts to assist new Baha'is and their families to adapt to the Baha'i rhythm of life and to deepen their knowledge of the Baha'i teachings.

3

Home and Family

My home is the home of peace. My home is the home of joy
and delight. My home is the home of laughter and exultation.
Whosoever enters through the portals of this home, must go out
with gladsome heart. This is the home of light; whosoever enters
here must become illumined . . .

'Abdu'l-Bahá, in Star of the West, *1918, p. 40*[4]

This description of the ideal Baha'i home as the nexus of all the
elements of the spiritual, physical, emotional, intellectual, educational and nurturing life of the individual, family and community
typifies the Baha'i approach to the interconnectedness of all aspects
of the religion and of life itself. The role of the home, and homemakers, both female and male, and of the family is central to the
Baha'i understanding of the purpose of life at the personal level and
in the wider community. The home depicted here is peaceful and
contributes to peace in society. It is happy and endows others with
that happiness. It is a place where true education, of the mind and
the soul, occurs and where the people who live in it and everyone
who comes into contact with it gains in wisdom and grows spiritually. There is energy, a zest for life itself, in such a home and living
there is exhilarating.

The Baha'i home is the focus of many of the activities associated
with Baha'i community life, including devotional gatherings, meetings where enquirers can learn about the religion, children's classes
and, in small Baha'i communities, 19-day feasts and holy day observances. Baha'is are urged to invite people of all backgrounds into their
homes and the offering of hospitality in one's home is a significant
aspect of Baha'i life.

The Baha'i home is at once the foundation of and the model for the
unified world society envisioned by Baha'u'llah. It provides the
seedbed and training ground for people who will foster unity at every
level of society and who will know how to live in, participate in and
govern such unified communities. The impetus towards unity is
acknowledged by Baha'is as the imperative of the present human
condition and the unity of humanity is the overarching thrust of the
teachings of Baha'u'llah. It is not surprising, then, that the unity of the

> Compare the nations of the world to the members of a family. A family is a nation in miniature. Simply enlarge the circle of the household, and you have the nation. Enlarge the circle of nations, and you have all humanity. The conditions surrounding the family surround the nation. The happenings in the family are the happenings in the life of the nation. Would it add to the progress and advancement of a family if dissensions should arise among its members, all fighting, pillaging each other, jealous and revengeful of injury, seeking selfish advantage? Nay, this would be the cause of the effacement of progress and advancement. So it is in the great family of nations, for nations are but an aggregate of families. Therefore, as strife and dissension destroy a family and prevent its progress, so nations are destroyed and advancement hindered. ('Abdu'l-Bahá, 1982, p. 157)

home and the family, which forms the basic unit of society, is taken so seriously by Baha'is and that they strive to embed within their homes and families the ethical values, attitudes, behaviours and practices that will inevitably be taken into the workplace, the community and, ultimately, into the international arena.

The beginning of unity for Baha'is is the unity of self – that is, the understanding that one is essentially a spiritual being; that the physical, emotional and intellectual aspects of the self are integrated with one's soul; and that the purpose of all aspects of life – physical, emotional and intellectual – is the spiritual advancement of one's soul before the death of the body. In relation to the home and family, therefore, a Baha'i living alone will still want to create in his or her home the same welcoming conditions of unity, peace, energy and life-enrichment that characterise the Baha'i ideal. At the same time, the Baha'i community will honour and respect the individual, ensure that arrangements for activities are appropriate for and accessible to everyone and seek to assist those who have children, are widowed, orphaned, ill or in need.

Marriage

So important is unity for the survival and progress of the world that every human relationship is predicated upon it. Thus Baha'u'llah encouraged his followers to marry as an 'assistance' to themselves and described marriage as a 'fortress for well-being and salvation' (Bahá'u'lláh in *Baha'i Prayers*, 2002, p. 118). For Baha'is, marriage is the commitment of a man and a woman to each other and is based on love, trust, loyalty and faithfulness. Without such commitment and faithfulness, the very basis of the higher unities of community, nation and the world is weakened and jeopardised. In keeping with the imperative of unity, Baha'u'llah requires that prospective marriage partners, of whatever age, seek the permission of their parents before marrying, thereby ensuring that the union of the marriage partners becomes also a union of families and thus at the very bottom of the pyramid of society there is a strong bond.

Marriage is considered an attachment of minds and hearts in both a physical and a spiritual union. The unity of husband and wife transcends their physical life together, if they have established spiritual bonds, and continues after their death. Marriage partners are to help each other improve their spiritual lives and create the conditions and environment within their marriage that enable each to contribute to the wider world.

A foundational principle of Baha'i marriage is the equality of women and men. The implications of this principle reach far beyond the home into the community, the workplace and eventually into international relations. Far from being a maxim that merely helps a couple determine who does what tasks in the family setting, this basic teaching of the Baha'i Faith is a driver of all the attitudes, behaviours and practices of the marriage partners in relationship to each other, to their children and to everyone else.

A significant purpose of marriage for Baha'is is to provide a channel for the 'proper use of the sex instinct' (Shoghi Effendi, 1938). The 'proper use' is within marriage only – there are no other circumstances in which Baha'is can legitimately have sexual relationships. While this stance is basically in line with those who uphold 'traditional morality', disapproving, as it does, of unbridled licence, Baha'is do not see sex as evil or 'dirty'. Baha'is are not ascetics and believe that sex, if properly used, can bring joy and satisfaction to an individual and his or her spouse and can greatly enhance one's life.

Baha'is are free to marry anyone they choose, whether Baha'i or not, and it is a feature of the Baha'i community that there are many marriages across ethnic, cultural, social, racial, national and religious heritages. The Baha'i community is well endowed with families of mixed parentage going back many generations and is familiar with the challenges that this may bring to individuals, families and communities. It is characteristic of Baha'is that they revel in such diversity and often actively encourage their children to seek marriage partners from a different background.

As with every other institution within the Baha'i community, decisions to be made by marriage partners are to be made by consultation and differences between them are to be resolved through the same process. Consultation not only allows decisions to be made and difficulties to be aired in a spiritual, dignified and courteous way, it also engenders unity and requires attitudes and behaviours that are useful in other settings, such as the workplace.

Should marriage partners be unable to resolve their differences, they are able to consult the local Baha'i institution, the local spiritual assembly, which is charged with the responsibility of assisting couples through such difficulties, encouraging them to have patience, helping them heal rifts and aiding them to re-establish unity, love and trust. Baha'is accept that not every marriage will succeed, particularly at a time when the social environment is not conducive to family life and society has not yet adopted the social principles that will enable it to function more effectively. Thus while divorce is discouraged, Baha'is are able to divorce, after waiting a year and engaging in the consultation process, and divorced Baha'is are able to remarry.

Children

An important purpose of Baha'i marriage is the procreation of children who will themselves be the embodiment of Baha'i values and Baha'i couples, if they are able, usually have children at some point in their married life.

> Enter into wedlock, O people, that ye may bring forth one who will make mention of Me amid My servants. *(Bahá'u'lláh, 1992, para. 63)*

Those who are unable to have their own often adopt or foster children, prompted by Baha'u'llah's statement: 'He that bringeth up his son or the son of another, it is as though he hath brought up a son of Mine' (Bahá'u'lláh, 1988b, p. 128).

The Baha'i teachings state that while the mother is 'the chief and primary educator of the children' and the father has 'the primary responsibility for the financial support of the family', it is expected that fathers will play a 'significant role in the education of the children' and that sometimes the mother may be the principal breadwinner in the family. The roles are not inflexibly fixed and can be changed and adjusted to suit particular family situations (Universal House of Justice, 1984c). In addition, the whole extended family as well as the Baha'i community itself may be involved in the education and raising of children. For example, the local spiritual assembly is to provide mothers with a programme for the education of children ('Abdu'l-

Bahá, 1978, p. 138). Teachers of children are honoured within the Baha'i community, even to the extent that Baha'is are encouraged to remember them in their wills, and the education of children is considered one of the most meritorious of deeds. Children are to be trained in spiritual values and attitudes and in literacy, sciences, arts, crafts and all subjects that conduce to human welfare and will advance civilisation. Parents and schools should teach children to sing and play music and also to give them a deep appreciation of it. Baha'i children are encouraged to take care of pets to teach them the importance of kindness to animals. 'Abdu'l-Baha indicated that the earliest years of a child's life are the most important and that the formal education of children should begin from the age of five ('Abdu'l-Bahá, in *Compilation*, 1991, vol. 1, p. 280). It is accepted, however, that children learn best from the example of others, particularly their parents, and that therefore the parents must strive to put the Baha'i values and ideals into practice at all times and to provide an environment in which children will thrive.

The values, attitudes, behaviours and practices that are the building blocks of the Baha'i home and family are the same as those found at every level of the Baha'i community. Values such as love, justice, honesty, trustworthiness, integrity, prizing the equality of women and men, honouring the intellect, and holding spiritual purity and detachment in high regard, form the moral backbone of individuals and their relationships at every level. Marriage partners endeavour to develop these qualities in themselves and to assist one another to secure them. They form the backdrop to the education of the children of the family and characterise the relationships that family members have with one another and with others.

Such moral principles shape the attitudes that individuals hold and a feature of the family will be the nurturing of attitudes that create and enrich opportunities to promote unity, justice and peace at all levels of society. Thus Baha'is are hopeful: they believe that people can change and that it is the purpose of religion to enable them to transform. Baha'is also place great emphasis on education as an agent of transformation, considering it to be a lifelong process that it is the responsibility of parents to begin with their children.

Regard man as a mine rich in gems of inestimable value. Education can, alone, cause it to reveal its treasures, and enable mankind to benefit therefrom. (Bahá'u'lláh, 1983, p. 260)

One of the unusual features of the Baha'i Faith is that girls have priority of education over boys if a family can only afford to educate some of its children. This is because the status of women, particularly as educators of the next generation, is enhanced in the religion and much importance is given to the teaching of its core values to children within a family setting. Thus the attitude to women, children, home-making and education is informed by the values outlined above and becomes the lynchpin of the transformation of society as well as of individuals.

Family Life

Baha'is believe that one of the attitudes necessary for a peaceful world is freedom from prejudice and that it is the role of parents not only to teach this to their children but to live it in their personal lives. Given the Baha'i teaching on the oneness of humanity, it is unsurprising that Baha'is are particularly concerned to root out racial prejudice, consid-ering it to be the 'most vital and challenging issue' confronting some countries (see Shoghi Effendi, 1990, pp. 33–41). Baha'is consider formal education itself to be a major factor in enabling people to relin-quish prejudices about race, ethnicity, religion and so on and Baha'i parents will want to ensure that schools and educational centres that their children attend foster the development of this attitude. Beyond this, a Baha'i family will take positive steps to provide opportunities for family members to mix with people from all backgrounds socially, to encourage spontaneous and informal association with them and to develop bonds of genuine friendship with a broad diversity of people. The example shown by parents in welcoming everyone into their own home and providing hospitality is the most powerful instrument to instil this attitude in children.

All such attitudes are derived from the basic Baha'i teaching about the nature of the human being as essentially spiritual. People's physi-cal characteristics are significant only to the extent that they lend their diversity to the beauty of the garden of humanity. Thus, the develop-ment of spiritual qualities in one's children, the nurturing of spiritual attitudes, helping children to see others as spiritual beings and to relate to them as such and the practice of behaviours that reflect this attitude are major undertakings in a Baha'i family.

Behaviour is intended to be the natural outcome of values and atti-tudes. For Baha'is, merely holding lofty ideals, while valuable to some degree, is insufficient. Unless such values and attitudes are reflected in one's own actions and relationships at all levels, and are sharpened and refined through practice, they are unable to influence the world in any significant way. Further, the behaviours such values and attitudes inspire are performed within society, not just on one's own. At the same time, the values and attitudes taught in the family can provide the front-line defence against harmful behaviours such as alcohol and substance abuse.

Among the most vital of many behaviours that derive from the values and attitudes that are engendered in Baha'i homes are those that have to do with the treatment of others. People are treated with respect because one understands the spiritual nature of the human being and therefore values each person, young and old. Girls and women are treated with equality and justice. Families living in communities in which women are traditionally restricted to the home encourage mothers to participate in the wider community, perhaps to work outside the home or to become social activists. Girls are given the same opportunity for education and advancement as boys and follow the same curriculum at school. Children have a right to education and parents have the responsibility to provide it. As indicated above, in those families that can afford to educate only a few of their children, girls are sent to school rather than boys, a practice with far-reaching implications. It is the responsibility of both parents to educate their children, to provide a home for their families and, in that sense, to be homemakers. Mothers are given a high status in Baha'i communities and, as noted above, are the primary educators of children in their early years, whereas a father who fails to educate his children forfeits the right of fatherhood. At the same time, Baha'i parents are encouraged to provide challenges for their children, to 'accustom them to hardship' and to teach them the importance of work, which in the Baha'i Faith is raised to the station of worship. Baha'is place a high value on literacy, particularly as this provides a person with direct access to the holy scriptures, which is fundamental to the independent investigation of truth which Baha'u'llah has enjoined. Further, Baha'is are to recite or read from their scriptures every morning and evening and literacy is key to this activity.

Baha'u'llah teaches that the tranquillity of the world and its order is dependent on justice, which is based on reward and punishment. Hence, Baha'i homes are disciplined but aspire to be violence free. The use of violence or even harsh words is eschewed in Baha'i families. All family members are expected to act with dignity, courtesy, justice and tranquillity towards everyone and to be treated in the same way.

The general atmosphere in the home is to be one of encouragement and a striving for excellence. Intellectual curiosity and a sense of discovery, of wonder and awe are to be cultivated. The home should be orderly, beautiful, clean and well organised and children and adults should have good manners.

> **Let them share in every new and rare and wondrous craft and art. Bring them up to work and strive, and accustom them to hardship. Teach them to dedicate their lives to matters of great import, and inspire them to undertake studies that will benefit mankind.** ('Abdu'l-Bahá, 1978, p. 129)

These ideals are not easy to achieve by families working in isolation and Baha'is look to the broader community, Baha'i and otherwise, to assist and provide moral support and for protection. For example, as Baha'i communities develop, the local assembly takes responsibility for the education of children if parents are unable to do this themselves. Baha'i local assemblies will usually offer the children of the community moral education and other classes to complement the education they receive at school and one of the three 'core' activities of Baha'i community development consists of simple children's classes open to all children, whether from Baha'i families or not. Baha'i families may always discuss issues with the local assembly and are urged to seek professional assistance when required.

As the quotation at the head of this chapter implies, humour and laughter are encouraged within Baha'i families and, along with prayer and worship, provide the oil that can ease relationships when things get difficult.

> I want you to be happy . . . to laugh, smile and rejoice in order that others may be made happy by you. *('Abdu'l-Baha, 1982, p. 218)*

Establishing values, attitudes and behaviours in oneself and one's family requires opportunities to practise them and there is no better location for such practice than in the family itself. Many of the practices found in the Baha'i community are first established within the family and are rehearsed there preliminary to their use in other contexts. On the other hand, many families try to implement practices they have learned from experience within the Baha'i community and this interdependence is advocated.

A basic skill that all Baha'is try to learn is consultation. This is far more than just a form of discussion and decision-making used by Baha'is within their administrative bodies and Baha'is are encouraged to use consultation when making personal or family decisions. Despite its difficulty, even young children can learn the basics of consultation at home and many families have formal or informal 'family consultations' to make decisions about such things as holidays, bedtimes and pocket money; as children get older, families may use consultation for more complex decisions. As mentioned above, couples use consultation, with some modification as there can be no 'majority', to make major decisions and to resolve differences between them. When agreement cannot be reached by the couple, it is expected that sometimes a husband will defer to his wife and at other times a wife will defer to her husband. Neither should ever dominate the other. Because Baha'is are encouraged to consult on all things, families may ask other family members, friends or other Baha'is to consult with them on decisions that are particularly challenging or that affect others. Consultation is a transferable skill and is useful in other settings, such as creating community cohesion and rebuilding neighbourhoods after disasters.

As noted above, Baha'u'llah has defined a new paradigm of work, stating that work done in the spirit of service to humanity is equated with worship. Further, he has counselled Baha'is to 'earn a livelihood by their calling' (Bahá'u'lláh, 1990, Persian 82). For Baha'is, there is a clear connection between education and work and between work and the prosperity of the individual, the family and the community. As discussed above, children are to be brought up to work and this can be effectively taught by parents in the home. Simple tasks such as feeding and grooming pets can be assigned even to quite young children and has the advantage of teaching them the Baha'i principle of kindness to animals. Since Baha'i households are to be orderly, children are encouraged to take pride in their home and, as they grow older, to take some responsibility for its care. Not only does this help them learn qualities of caring, helpfulness and trustworthiness, it also gives them a sense of accomplishment and achievement and they learn the value of their own actions – other lessons that will benefit them and others as they move from the family into school, work and the community.

The development of a devotional attitude is a central aspiration of every Baha'i. At the community level, Baha'is participate in a number of activities that foster this condition, including 19-day feasts and, ultimately, gatherings in the Baha'i house of worship. Baha'i families are encouraged to pray together and parents are to teach their children simple prayers and verses from Baha'i scripture. Many parents say prayers with their children when they get up in the morning and when they go to bed at night. As there are no formal postures to adopt in prayer and no particular gestures, other than for obligatory prayers, families are free to find their own ways to worship together. Increasingly, Baha'i families invite neighbours, friends and relatives to join them in weekly or monthly devotional gatherings. Such gatherings not only help develop the devotional condition, they also teach children hospitality and give them a practical example of how prejudices can be relinquished as people from all backgrounds are welcomed into the home.

The Baha'i Faith has no clergy and no people responsible for its propagation other than ordinary Baha'is themselves. Thus each Baha'i is charged with the duty of 'teaching' the Faith to others.[5] There are many ways to do this but Baha'is are particularly urged to open their homes to people wishing to learn about the Baha'i Faith to discuss some aspect of the religion, offer them hospitality and answer their questions. These 'firesides' are to be held at least once every 19 days. This practice not only enables people to learn more about the Baha'i teachings but also provides an opportunity for them to see how Baha'is live their lives. Increasingly, Baha'is are participating in study circles through which they increase and deepen their knowledge of their religion. Many study circles are held in private homes and these have proved to be another avenue by which people are introduced to the Baha'i Faith. In addition, when their parents host firesides and study circles, the children of the home are set a powerful example of Baha'i behaviour. This reinforces their basic education within the Baha'i Faith and helps establish the rhythm of their Baha'i lives.

Baha'is see important links between the family, education, children, homemaking, work, the status of women, the equality of women and men and the advancement of society. Thus, for example, both women and men are responsible for aspects of homemaking and for creating the conditions in the home that foster the education of children and keep them healthy. This has implications not only for the family but for the workplace and the community, both of which need to change to enable both parents to nurture their children and to provide the environment in which families can thrive. Similarly, the attitude of society towards women who work and men who look after children also needs to change. These changes are made more possible by the entry into the community of children who have already had opportunities to practise these attitudes and behaviours in the home. Such changes in society, Baha'is believe, will uplift the welfare and prosperity of humanity at large and enhance the probability of long-term political stability and peace. While these expectations may appear grandiose, they are drivers of Baha'i life at all levels.

4

Living in the Community

Be generous in prosperity, and thankful in adversity.
Be worthy of the trust of thy neighbour, and look
upon him with a bright and friendly face.

Bahá'u'lláh, 1983, p. 285

Just as Baha'is strive to create families that are united, just and peaceful, they try to translate the same ethical values and attitudes taught by Baha'u'llah into behaviours and practices that will foster unity and harmony in the villages, towns and cities where they live – recognising that without such unity, no community, however prosperous or advanced, can survive. At the most basic level, Baha'is endeavour to be good neighbours and useful citizens and try to contribute positively to the well-being and concord of their neighbourhoods.

Far from being aloof, Baha'is are very much a part of the local communities in which they reside. They are generally active participants in programmes designed to increase community cohesion, to foster harmony among neighbours, to combat racism and to provide humanitarian assistance and welfare. Many Baha'is are involved in local environmental projects and in programmes that work to advance the status of women or to provide youth with worthwhile sporting and leisure activities. Others assist campaigns that promote literacy and often work to improve local amenities. Baha'is are ardent supporters of interfaith activities. Many Baha'is volunteer to serve in lay capacities as magistrates or on public health bodies. In those parts of the world where local government authorities are unable to provide education, health or social services, Baha'is have often established projects to provide these, sometimes with other people and agencies. Baha'is may also offer courses designed to promote wealth creation, such as market gardening, handicrafts and sewing, and many of these are aimed particularly at women and girls. In some places classes on child rearing, nutrition and home-making are provided and most Baha'i communities offer moral education classes for children and programmes on how to teach virtues for adults.

The Baha'i Faith sets out a vision of a united world community, based on spiritual principles such as love and justice and functioning for the benefit of all people. Baha'is believe such a united world is not a pious hope but an imperative towards which steps must be – and are being – taken. Thus they see Baha'u'llah's writings as providing the practical measures that will enable humanity to progress to this point. They believe that world unity is itself built on peaceful, strong and united countries, which in turn requires communities that are themselves healthy, united and flourishing. Such communities are dependent on the basic units of society, families, for their own sustainability. At the same time, Baha'is recognise that society has a long way to travel before such a vision can be realised and that, at every level, the commitment, talents and hard work of individuals and their governments will be required for progress to be made.

The Baha'i Vision of Cohesive Communities

Baha'is envision the emergence of truly cohesive communities that 'promote human dignity, stimulate the release of human potential, and actively cultivate the inherent nobility which Baha'is believe makes up the basis of human nature' (National Spiritual Assembly of the United Kingdom, 2002). Baha'u'llah's teachings describe communities with a closely-knit social fabric based on shared spiritual and moral values and the active cooperation of all citizens, who will have a genuine concern for each other.

Baha'is maintain that the key to establishing strong, peaceful and prosperous communities is to develop those elements that tend to create social cohesion and to work to overcome the prejudices, fears, distrust, injustices and deprivations that tear communities apart. Even identifying these elements is a major task in itself, while the work required to address them needs to be undertaken sensitively, wisely and urgently. Baha'is recognise that just as it is challenging for family members to learn to live together in harmony, so neighbourhoods and communities will also find it a difficult and delicate task to create and maintain cohesion and concord.

Baha'is believe that communities should value and serve everyone living in them, not just those who are well off, educated or privileged in some way. Many towns and cities today are composed of people from a variety of nationalities, backgrounds, cultures, religious traditions and ethnicities, and social, economic, legal and political systems should reflect and respect this diversity. Legislation alone, important as it is, cannot create the social climate in which different communities can offer their own skills and talents to the whole. A truly cohesive and equitable society requires people who understand that the interests of individuals and the community are intertwined, that the securing of human and civil rights requires a commitment to their corresponding responsibilities and that both women and men must participate fully in decision-making and planning.

Coupled with the need to create cohesive communities is the need to develop sustainable patterns of living within the community setting. Baha'is believe that the natural environment requires the same sensitive and wise care that people expect for themselves and that the built environment should reflect not only the physical needs of the community but also its spiritual and aesthetic ones. Hence Baha'is advocate that beauty as well as utility should be incorporated into community development plans.

Meeting the Challenge

To achieve such communities, Baha'is actively promote a consciousness and appreciation of the oneness of the human family. In the absence of such an understanding, Baha'is note that governments and communities have been hindered in their attempts to overcome the sorts of tensions and fears that create civil unrest. Thus Baha'is urge individuals and families to associate with people of different beliefs, customs and outlooks, as well as with people of different ethnic and racial backgrounds, so that they may learn to value the diversity of their communities and replace fearful ignorance with understanding and knowledge. They also recommend that work places offer training courses on this subject. They consider it to be essential not only that schools include programmes that provide such opportunities for their pupils but also that an integral part of school curricula be the teaching of the oneness of humanity and a sense of world citizenship. In addition, where feasible, Baha'is themselves seek to participate in and influence the processes of community development so that their communities are shaped around the same spiritual values of love, trustworthiness, justice, equality and integrity that underpin Baha'i home life.

Baha'is accept that increasing interaction among people of different backgrounds and their growing interdependence 'poses fundamental challenges to traditional ways of thinking and acting' and that it is how individuals and communities respond to these challenges that 'will, to a large degree, determine whether our communities become nurturing, cohesive and progressive, or inhospitable, divided and unsustainable' (Bahá'í International Community, 1996b).

The Role of Religion

Baha'is believe religion itself has a significant role to play in creating harmonious and cohesive communities. However, too often religion is itself the cause of tensions and disturbances, having been perverted to turn neighbour against neighbour. Religion has been responsible for wars, bloodshed and much human suffering.

Baha'is accept that fanaticism and extremism – which they consider to be corruptions of true religion – have destroyed tolerance and poisoned communities. Some sectarian leaders have discouraged investigation of other beliefs or have spoken out against the followers of other religions. Baha'is consider that such attitudes not only foster prejudice but have led to the sometimes violent attacks on believers of other faiths, thus undermining the very spiritual values religion purports to uphold.

If there is to be a constructive dialogue about the role of religion in establishing social justice in communities, Baha'is believe this history must be acknowledged and religious leaders must themselves eschew religious intolerance, violence and terrorism and seek rather to focus on the commonly shared spiritual principles of all religions. Religious leaders themselves will need to work to expel religious bigotry and superstition from within their faith traditions and will have to accept freedom of conscience for all people, including their own followers. Baha'is believe that it is the responsibility of religious leaders to make it clear to their followers that prejudice, bigotry and violence have no place in the life of a religious person. However, Baha'is expect religious leaders to go further: 'Denunciations of materialism or terrorism are of no real assistance in coping with the contemporary moral crisis if they do not begin by addressing candidly the failure of responsibility that has left believing masses exposed and vulnerable to these influences' (Universal House of Justice, 2002).

If religion can redeem itself, Baha'is believe it holds the key to creating spiritually-centred communities that fulfil the vision Baha-'u'llah set out for them. 'Religion is the greatest of all means for the establishment of order in the world and for the peaceful contentment of all that dwell therein' (Bahá'u'lláh, quoted in Shoghi Effendi, 1991, p. 186).

When it has been faithful to the spirit and example of the transcendent Figures who gave the world its great belief systems, it has awakened in whole populations capacities to love, to forgive, to create, to dare greatly, to overcome prejudice, to sacrifice for the common good and to discipline the impulses of animal instinct. Unquestionably, the seminal force in the civilizing of human nature has been the influence of the succession of these Manifestations of the Divine that extends back to the dawn of recorded history. *(Universal House of Justice, 2002)*

Baha'is consider that one of the most important ways in which religious leaders can foster harmony and stimulate cooperation and dialogue among their followers is to encourage them to seek out religious truth for themselves. All religions teach that truth need not be feared. If 'people of religious faith believe that the Creator is eternal and the centre of all existence, then they must also believe that the unfettered and genuine search for truth will lead to truth' (Bahá'í International Community, 2001b).

Influencing Decision-Makers

Baha'is envision that the universal recognition of the oneness of humanity will implement an 'organic change in the structure of present-day society' (Shoghi Effendi, 1991, p. 43) and they both advocate and actively support the sorts of social initiatives that will profit the whole of society. However, Baha'is consider that partisan politics is not a beneficial way of achieving this and they themselves do not join political parties, run for office, or canvas for political parties or individual politicians. They may and do vote in elections when they can do so without identifying themselves with a particular political party and they may also serve in government positions that are not party political. Baha'is are loyal and obedient to the government under which they live and do not criticise or try to undermine it. Where governments solicit the views of civil society and where it is legally possible to make representations to the government to change policy or legislation, the national spiritual assembly of that country may do so if the occasion arises and the Baha'is have something relevant to say. Hence, for example, the National Spiritual Assembly of the United Kingdom has responded to requests from the British government for comments on a variety of topics, from human rights to education.

Similarly, at the local level, local spiritual assemblies may offer their views on a variety of local issues and many are engaged in such initiatives as Local Agenda 21 and other environmental projects, community safety and crime reduction. However, Baha'is do not resort to tactics such as street demonstrations or other forms of aggressive public action to put across their points of view.

Developing United, Spiritualised, Sustainable Communities

When Baha'i communities reach a high level of maturation and partici-pation, they are often able to implement programmes of social and economic development that serve their neighbourhoods or the wider community and foster Baha'u'llah's vision of a united, just, prosperous and peaceful world civilisation. In recent years, many Baha'i-inspired organisations have developed to stimulate discussion of Baha'i ideas and to promote their application to a range of social, humanitarian, legal and economic issues. In addition, many such organisations do practical field work using Baha'i teachings as the framework for their values and mission.

For Baha'is, material development cannot be successful unless it is linked with spiritual development and the implementation of values, thus Baha'i-inspired organisations and projects are underpinned by the values found in the teachings of Baha'u'llah. Many of the social teachings of the Baha'i Faith are central to development issues: the need for unity and a recognition of the oneness of humanity, universal education, the equality of women and men, the abolition of the extremes of wealth and poverty, the implementation of social and economic justice, the need for ethical governance and the need for universal participation in social action. Among the most effective programmes of social development are those that focus on raising the status of women and enabling women and girls to obtain an educa-tion, particularly literacy. At present, there are some two thousand such projects and Baha'i-inspired organisations across the world and the examples below are merely illustrative of their range and variety.

Barli Vocational Institute for Rural Women, Indore, India

Established in 1985, the Barli Vocational Institute for Rural Women was set up to train rural and tribal women from villages around Indore in the skills and knowledge they need to improve their quality of life and that of their families and communities by initiating development activities that will improve health and nutrition, raise household income, increase literacy and protect and improve the environment. *Barli* is the local word for the central pillar of the house and the Insti-tute is founded on the principle that like the *barli* that supports the structure of the building, women support the structure of the family and the community. All of the training programmes, which last from six months to a year, are free of charge to women, who come mainly from tribal areas.

A main focus is to facilitate change in the traditional attitudes and practices that block or impede the efforts of women and men to live in equality with dignity and security. The courses particularly seek to overcome obstacles that have hindered the development of women, providing women with opportunities to reflect on the nature of their relationships with others and with their social institutions. They examine caste, tribal and class prejudices in the light of Baha'i principles, while identifying positive elements in their culture that need to be preserved and strengthened.

Training courses are taught holistically and include literacy, tailoring, agriculture, artisan craftwork, human rights, environmental awareness, self-esteem and personality development, social commitment, nutrition and health, and income-generating skills. Art, music and dance are also incorporated into the curriculum. The objective is that, once empowered with such training, the women can return to their home villages and become the *barli* of their families and communities, agents for changing the social and physical environments.

Radio Baha'i, Ecuador

Radio Baha'i, Ecuador, located 95 km north of Quito in Otavalo, was conceived as a way to keep members of the quickly growing Baha'i community in touch with one another, but it rapidly emerged as a community radio station serving a wide indigenous population and became the primary link among *campesinos* (country people) across the region. Its programming, which is in both the local Quichua and Spanish languages, reflects the interests and culture of the *campesinos* and focuses on their spiritual and moral well-being as well as on the social and economic development of the area. Hence, it promotes education and provides basic information about health, social issues and development.

An important element of Radio Baha'i's programming is the sharing of news about activities taking place in the area. A particularly useful programme is a sort of 'lost and found', which looks for missing people, animals and possessions.

The heart of Radio Baha'i's popularity is its support for traditional Andean music, other traditional arts and crafts and local folklore. Indigenous culture is often overwhelmed by European and North American imports and local languages and cultures quickly become marginalised or even vanish. Radio Baha'i reinforces the positive culture of the indigenous Quichua people and has reversed their decline.

In addition, Radio Baha'i has been a training ground for local people, many of them illiterate, who operate the station and prepare and front its programmes and who have gone on to train others. This has helped establish the legitimacy of the station in the region and has reinforced its popularity.

Radio Baha'i Ecuador has become a model for similar radio stations in other parts of the world, including the United States, as well as Bolivia, Chile, Panama and Peru.

Ocean of Light International School, Tonga

The Ocean of Light International School on the outskirts of Nuku'alofa, Tonga in the South Pacific has become well known for its high standard of moral and academic education and for the treatment of its students. Based on the Baha'i belief that education should produce people who are willing to work towards serving others as well as striving towards creating an ever advancing civilisation, the Ocean of Light School is dedicated to the development of the spiritual, intellectual and physical potential of its students and to world citizenship. The school opened in 1996 with nine pupils and two teachers but less than a decade later provides education from kindergarten through high school for nearly 300 children from seven nationalities. It is the first school in Tonga to offer internationally recognised examinations (Cambridge International Exams).

The Baha'i Faith teaches that the development of character is the foundation for success in life and Baha'is believe that a good character is even more important than achievement in the academic sphere. Thus from the beginning, in addition to the Tongan national curriculum, the school has taught virtues to every student, not merely as fine words but as practical tools for daily living. As a result, the school is well known for the good behaviour of its children and for teachers who are good role models of honesty, kindness, thoughtfulness, compassion, trustworthiness and hard work. The school promotes a different sort of relationship between teachers and the students than is generally found in Tongan schools, a relationship that is characterised by spiritual principles, is less autocratic and more egalitarian and is based on a system of cooperative discipline rather than corporal punishment.

The aim of the school is to prepare children to live in the emerging global society which, Baha'is believe, will require the spiritual values, attitudes, behaviours and practices outlined in the Baha'i teachings. Although only about a fifth of the students come from Baha'i families and most of the teachers are not themselves Baha'is, the school is committed to educating children so that they will be capable of participating in the construction of the new world order envisaged by Baha'u'llah. To achieve this, the school seeks to develop in its pupils the spirit of service to others, as well as 'the capacities, skills, habits and attitudes necessary to enable them to provide for their families; to effectively contribute to the peace, prosperity and tranquillity of humanity; and to participate in the creation of new institutions, processes and relationships as they are defined and established' (Ocean of Light website).

European Baha'i Business Forum (EBBF)

In 1989 the international economic scene changed dramatically with the ending of the Cold War, the opening up of eastern and central Europe and the dawning of a global economy. In 1990 a group of Baha'is active in business and management met in France to discuss how to respond positively to the changed environment and to reverse the decline of ethics and values in business. From their discussions was born the European Baha'i Business Forum (EBBF), a network of like-minded business people that promotes the moral and spiritual wisdom and principles of the great religious traditions of the world, including the Baha'i Faith. Now located in over 50 countries, EBBF has become an influential organisation, with a wide range of publications, that works in collaboration with other networks and organisations holding similar values.

Initially, the main work of EBBF was to translate the Baha'i spiritual ideals into a language that people in business would accept and treat seriously. Its first publication, *Emerging Values for a Global Economy*, highlighted how ethical principles could be used in the new economic environment. EBBF advocates a set of core values derived from the Baha'i teachings: business ethics, corporate social responsibility, sustainable development, partnership of women and men, a new paradigm of work, consultation in decision-making and values-based leadership. Members of EBBF try to incorporate these core values into their own working lives and businesses and encourage their implementation by colleagues.

As the organisation has developed it has taken on a wider role, for instance collaborating with the International Labour Organisation to produce a joint working paper on 'Socially Responsible Enterprise Restructuring' that has been published in English and Russian, with condensed versions in French, Italian and Polish. A significant development was the establishment in 2002 at the University of Bari, Italy, of a Chair for the Study of the New World Order, which teaches an EBBF-inspired programme on economics and business. The programme was quickly replicated in universities across Italy and EBBF now provides a Master's degree programme as well as undergraduate courses.

From its early days EBBF has concentrated on eastern and central Europe, co-sponsoring a business ethics conference annually in Bulgaria and co-publishing with the *Albanian Economic Tribune* a series of seven articles on entrepreneurship.

EBBF has always focused on young people, offering a mentorship programme to young professionals and advice on careers and ethics to students. It is partnered with AIESEC, the business student organisation, and provides speakers on topics related to values-based leadership (see www.ebbf.org).

Vegetable Gardening in Mongolia

After the collapse of the centralised state in Mongolia in 1993, the diet of local people declined to such an extent that by 1997 the Human Development Report for Mongolia, published by the United Nations Development Programme (UNDP), identified the lack of vegetables as contributing significantly to the vitamin deficiency that was causing 'diseases and disorders', many of which were not reversible, and stunting growth in children. The traditional nomadic diet of meat and dairy products and a short growing season, coupled with the withdrawal of state support after the Soviet regime, severely restricted the consumption of fruit and vegetables. So worried was the Mongolian government that it instituted a nationwide project to increase the production of wheat and other crops.

At the same time, the newly established Baha'i community in the small, remote village of Erdenbulgan in northern Mongolia decided that they wanted to do something together that would assist the village. Starting from the idea that whatever project they undertook should serve the wider community and contribute to its welfare, the Baha'is considered various possibilities. After consultation it was decided that planting their own community garden to grow fresh vegetables, although they had never seen or eaten them before, would be the most feasible and the most needed. They got permission from the local government to fence off land and called upon the expertise of a nearby Baha'i to train them, as they had no experience at all in vegetable growing.

They threw themselves into the project energetically, with even the younger members of the community helping keep watch on the garden 24 hours a day, often staying up all night in the tool shed on the site to do so. The garden has produced hundreds of kilos of vegetables previously unknown to local people, who have developed a taste for them and have developed their own recipes.

As well as contributing to the health of local people, the Erden-bulgan garden project soon became a model for the area of how to take community action. The project uses consultation as a way to make decisions and to take collective action and it involves the whole community working in unity, children and elderly included. It also created a breakthrough in thinking. Under the communists, local gardens were prohibited as they were regarded as private enterprise and people, traditionally unused to eating vegetables in any case, thought the climate and soil of Mongolia made the growing of vegetables very difficult. The Erdenbulgan garden project showed that, with determination and people working together in unity, vegetable growing is possible. They have also learned the skills of community development which can be translated to other projects.

Volunteer Community Health Workers, Uganda

A small health project begun by the Baha'i community in north-east Uganda in 1986 has become a model of sustainability, and its success has been ascribed to its incorporation of many of Baha'u'llah's key social principles: work done in the spirit of service is worship, gender equality, consultation and unity of action. The project focuses on the vaccination of children and on promoting sanitation and hygienic practices among villagers and is carried out by volunteers from the community itself.

The Uganda Baha'i Institute for Development (UBID) trains local volunteers to be community health workers and vaccinators. They in turn teach other villagers about sanitation and hygiene and vaccinate children against the main childhood diseases. Local health education trainers work with and support the volunteers. UBID was initially financed locally, but in 1993 it received a grant from the Canadian Public Health Association to help it extend its training programme.

Unusually for such a project, almost half the trained volunteers have been women, reversing the traditional pattern of women working only in the home. Convinced of Baha'u'llah's teaching on the equality of women and men, the Baha'i community believed it was important to the success of the project to have gender balance among the volunteers and much effort was spent recruiting, training and encouraging women. For example, the training programme was arranged so that women could bring their babies and young children with them. Similarly, a great effort was made to overcome the objection of husbands, who were initially opposed to their wives taking part. However, when the men saw the beneficial changes to their own lives that the training brought, they acquiesced.

It was largely due to the fact of using local people that the project even got off the ground. Villagers were suspicious that the vaccinations might kill the children rather than protect them and it was only because the volunteer health workers came from their own villages that they brought their children for immunisation. The health workers first vaccinated their own children, thereby demonstrating the safety and value of the procedure and winning the confidence of their fellow-villagers.

Using bicycles and motorbikes, the volunteer community health workers travel to the remotest parts of the district where health services are scarce. Over the years, they have helped to raise immunisation rates significantly and to decrease child mortality in 30 villages across the whole of eastern Uganda.

Swindon Youth Empowerment Project, United Kingdom

When the Spiritual Assembly of Swindon, United Kingdom, consulted about what the local community needed and how the Baha'is could best serve those needs, it identified young people as a population whose potential was not fully realised. The Baha'i community was already involved in a number of other activities based around a 'Tranquillity Zone', an initiative of the Baha'i community in the United Kingdom in which a spiritual atmosphere is created in a specially created 'room', draped with flowing curtains, furnished with comfortable cushions, decorated with flowers and elegantly lit with candles, in which the scriptures are read and music played. It was decided that the Tranquillity Zone could form the heart of a project that would empower young people, assist them in a process of self-discovery and help them to develop a sense of purpose, personal responsibility and service. Thus the 'Youth Empowerment Project' was born in 2001.

Young people are referred to the project from social services, the probation service, schools and other organisations that work with youth and the Swindon Baha'is work in partnership with youth agencies to provide the eight-week course. Many of the young people referred to the project describe themselves as angry, suicidal, depressed or bored and often come from disturbed backgrounds or environments in which they are made to feel that they are worthless, troublemakers or 'bad' and that there is no value or point to their lives.

Every week for eight weeks groups of young people enter a specially designed Tranquillity Zone. There they experience a different world of stories and music in the beautiful tent-like environment where they can relax and learn visualisation techniques. From the Tranquillity Zone, they move on to the Discovery Zone, a series of interactive workshops designed to enable the young people to begin to discover their true selves. Here they learn the importance of spiritual qualities such as love, kindness, patience and wisdom, and how these fit into their lives. They learn that they have a spiritual nature and that they are able to make choices about their own actions and direct their own lives. Stories related in the Tranquillity Zone form the basis for discussion in the Discovery Zone, while a variety of activities enable the young people to learn about their higher selves, to discover their own potential and to understand what leads to happiness and unhappiness.

While at first some of the young people have a negative attitude towards the project and treat it as a joke, most persevere and eventually attend the sessions with enthusiasm. Gradually they begin to learn not only that they are valuable human beings but that they have something to offer to others, which puts them on a path of service rather than self-destruction. In Level 2 of the programme the young people undertake their own acts of service, for instance by offering Tranquillity Zones to their friends and families.

The project also provides training for the volunteer facilitators in the Training Zone, giving them the skills, insights and knowledge necessary to run Tranquillity Zones and Youth Empowerment courses. In the Training Zone volunteers learn how to relate to youth and how to create an atmosphere of trust. They learn the effective use of speaking, silence and music and how to bring peace to agitated young people. At the same time, volunteers learn much about themselves and about human nature.

So successful is the project that it has attracted funding from a variety of sources, including the European Social Fund, the Learning and Skills Council and the Partnership Development Fund.

Tahirih Justice Center, United States

Based in Washington DC, the Tahirih Justice Center, a Baha'i-inspired organisation, was created following a high-profile asylum case in 1997 (see Kassindja and Miller Bashir, 1998). Layli Miller-Muro, then a newly qualified lawyer, had successfully won a landmark case for a woman fleeing a regime of genital mutilation in her own country. The case changed US law and made it possible for women seeking asylum for gender-based persecution to enter the United States. Following the case, so many women sought Ms Miller-Muro's advice and assistance that she decided to set up a not-for-profit, Baha'i-inspired organisation that could meet their needs. The principle underpinning the organisation is the Baha'i belief that the advancement of civilisation depends on the actualisation of the equality of women and men.

The Justice Center is named after Tahirih, a famous 19th-century Iranian scholar and poet who was an ardent follower of the Bab, the forerunner to Baha'u'llah. She was an early champion of women's rights who was executed for her beliefs in 1852, saying 'You can kill me as soon as you like, but you cannot stop the emancipation of women' (Shoghi Effendi, 1995, p. 75).

The Center was set up to protect women from human rights abuses, such as trafficking and female genital mutilation, and its mission is to enable women and girls who face gender-based violence and persecution to have access to justice. To fulfil this mission it undertakes litigation but also engages in advocacy on public policy, education and outreach activities, a holistic approach based on the recognition that 'the attainment of freedom from persecution under the law is only the first step in helping women realise the attainment of justice and well-being in their lives'. Much of the work is undertaken by volunteers, offering their time pro bono. In the early days, most the volunteers were under 30 years old and had full-time legal careers.

The Tahirih Justice Center recognises, as indicated in the Baha'i writings, that only an organic change in society – in this case, the legal environment – will be sufficient to ensure the protection of women and girls from violence and guarantee their human rights in the long term. Thus, the advocacy work of the Center seeks to influence decision-makers and focuses on changing public policy legislation.

The Center's outreach programme provides women with medical assistance, psychological care and social services, using volunteer doctors and psychiatrists and social workers. The Center also trains the police, workers at women's refuges and social workers.

In 2002 the Tahirih Justice Center launched a 'Campaign to End Exploitation by International Marriage Brokers', after discovering that the mail-order bride industry was marrying 'traditional' wives to abusive men. The campaign aims to create legislation that will regulate the industry, make businesses accountable and require disclosure of a man's criminal records and marital background to prospective brides.

The Center fields about 50 telephone calls a week from women seeking assistance. By 2004 the Center had assisted more than 5,000 women and girls (www.tahirih.org).

APRODEPIT, Chad

One of the primary concerns of people living along the Chair River in southern Chad has been the decline in the number of fish over the years. Whereas once fish were abundant, by the turn of the century they had all but disappeared. Water levels in rivers and lakes had dropped dramatically and local people continued to use harmful practices, such as the use of dynamite to kill fish. Overfishing and small-holed nets contributed to the problem. At the same time, there was great need to increase the amount of protein eaten by the local people. To address these issues the Baha'i-inspired national non-governmental organisation APRODEPIT (Action pour la Promotion des Ressources des Organisations de Défense de l'Environnement et de la Pisciculture integrée au Tchad: Action for the Promotion of Resources for Organisations Defending the Environment and Integrated Pisciculture in Chad) was created to promote community-based, environmentally sound development practices. APRODEPIT was the inspiration of Kosse Malla, a Baha'i who decided to put into practice his belief in the importance of service to others.

Rather than using expensive outside agencies to tackle the problem, APRODEPIT relies on local knowledge and local people themselves. Its main aim is to show communities how they can develop themselves. Its approach to development is based on the Baha'i method of consultation, the belief in the equality of women and men and stewardship of the environment. Local community groups – the communities usually decide to have one for men and another for women – are established that consult about what is needed and then APRODEPIT tries to match that need by enabling people to solve their own problems. It provides training for local people in sustainable fishing, fish farming and the preservation of fish through smoking and curing. It also promotes composting, arboriculture, reforestation and the protection of wildlife. APRODEPIT recognises, however, that other important issues concern the local population. It considers that these issues are all interrelated and require a holistic approach. Thus it also assists local people to educate their children, deal with health issues and tackle illiteracy, particularly among women.

Using participatory methods found in the Baha'i teachings, APRODEPIT has helped almost 200 villages in the region and around the capital city. Many of the practices advocated are basic and very simple. For example, because of the decline in the fish population, local fisherman made nets using a micromesh to catch immature fish because there were so few larger ones. This depleted the stocks even further, but little was done to prevent it. A community-based group of about 70 fishermen decided to reject the small-holed nets in favour of more traditional wide-meshed ones, with the result that fish stocks began to increase.

In Waltama, a village with a community group since 1995, villagers have instituted sustainable fishing, opened a school, created a village granary and provide literacy classes for women. One idea that emerged from their consultation was to create a protected wildlife area for hippopotamuses. They discovered that there were more fish where hippos lived and therefore they decided it was important to protect them. They now keep watch on the designated stretch of the river and drive poachers away. This has increased the hippo population from two in 1995 to about 200 and has increased the number of fish: the hippo manure attracts small insects which in turn feed the fish.

The government points to these community groups as models of how sustainable development can occur, remarking on the huge difference it makes when local knowledge is considered to be valuable rather than something to be ignored or eliminated. People act more effectively, government officials note, when they consider themselves to be partners in a plan rather than observers.

5

Social Issues

The Great Being saith: O ye children of men! The fundamental
purpose animating the Faith of God and His Religion is to safeguard
the interests and promote the unity of the human race, and to foster the
spirit of love and fellowship amongst men.

Bahá'u'lláh, 1983, p. 215

. . . the purpose of religion is the acquisition of praiseworthy virtues, the
betterment of morals, the spiritual development of mankind,
the real life and divine bestowals.

'Abdu'l-Bahá, 1982, p. 152

Be anxiously concerned with the needs of the age ye live in, and centre
your deliberations on its exigencies and requirements.

Bahá'u'lláh, 1983, p. 213

For Baha'is, religion is intended to be an instrument both for the
spiritual transformation, development and refinement of the individual
and for the reformation, improvement and advancement of humanity
as a whole. These two objectives are intertwined. Baha'is believe, on the
one hand, that it is not possible for individuals to achieve their highest
spiritual development in an environment that is hostile to this and, on
the other, that the truly spiritually evolved individual has a powerful,
uplifting effect on the community. Equally, the advancement of the
whole community is dependent on the spiritual development of its
individual members and individuals progress spiritually in communities
that support their spiritual progress.

Thus Baha'is consider that the destiny of humanity collectively is
bound up with the spiritual efforts and achievements of individuals.
That is, one's personal salvation is bound up with the salvation of the
world and individuals have a responsibility to assist in the advancement of the world as well as to uplift themselves.

Baha'is anticipate and work for the evolution of a world community that is rich in the diversity of its citizens, united, peaceful, just and
prosperous. They posit that the governance of the world community
will be a federal government determined by democratic processes at
local, national and international levels. Far from diminishing the

importance of the individual in such a united world, people are valued individually for their unique contributions, their rights are protected and each person is to be enabled to develop his or her own potential – materially, spiritually, intellectually and emotionally – to the highest degree.

The efforts of individuals and communities to establish such a world also provides them with the attitudes, skills and behaviours that are required to live in that world community. The very act of working with others towards this goal provides people with the insights and abilities that are useful for sustaining such a community. Further, these are the same insights and attitudes that are required by individuals for their own spiritual advancement and so, in this way, the two elements of individual development and collective progress are also entwined. Hence, it is the Baha'i belief that such personal devotional practices such as prayer and devotions, which are linked to transformation in the life of the individual through the development of spiritual qualities such as love, justice, patience and detachment, need to be reflected in one's interactions with others and that, ultimately, these qualities need to emerge at the community, national and international levels.

At the same time, Baha'is recognise that there is a profound interrelationship between the material and spiritual aspects of life (see Universal House of Justice, 1984b) and that progress in the social and economic dimensions of civilisation is dependent on the values that underpin it. These values can be oriented towards the welfare of others – justice, honesty, trustworthiness and so on – or they can be focused on a narrower self-interest – 'me first', the acquisition of personal wealth, power, ambition and the like. For Baha'is, 'the spiritual precedes the material' (Universal House of Justice, 1984a), that is, individuals are first illumined by spiritual teachings and these inspire them and give them the ability to effect beneficial material change in their communities. One consequence of this is that Baha'is do not believe that the social problems facing the world can be solved merely by social or economic means. The disparity between the rich and poor countries of the world, for example, cannot be resolved merely by a redistribution of wealth, better education, more equitable trading arrangements or by a more effective management of resources, desirable as all those are. The social problems that the world faces are, according to Baha'i belief, fundamentally spiritual problems and thus their solutions must also be spiritual. Greed, hatred, arrogance, dishonesty and a disregard for others are the basis of the world's social problems and these are essentially spiritual problems that will only yield to spiritual solutions.

The primary spiritual solution that needs to be applied is an appreciation of the unity of rank and station of all people and the behaviours that derive from this understanding. The concept that all people are equal is a difficult one to grasp and elusive in practice. This is because the world is constructed on a completely different principle – that people are *not* equal in status – and thus fundamental to the social problems facing the world is the hierarchical nature of the society in which we all live. All aspects of our human lives are dominated by hierarchical structures: government, business, most occupations, the educational world, even our recreational world and often our family life. For more than 6,000 years human beings have lived within these hierarchical, hegemonic structures and so this has become a deeply ingrained part of our thinking. In other words, it has become part of our concept of reality – it is normal and natural for us to live in hierarchical social structures.

The values that support hierarchical structures reflect the nature of hierarchies, which is to be highly competitive, with rewards going to those who win and reach the top of the hierarchy and little or nothing for those who fail. Power, wealth and victory are thus the highest values and the ultimate measure of success in such structures; weakness, poverty and failure are looked down upon. Those who have power and wealth are listened to and their needs are met; they are allowed to fulfil their potential and their deeds are recorded in newspapers and books. Those who do not possess power and wealth are ignored, and their needs remain unfulfilled; their potential remains undeveloped, their actions unrecorded and forgotten. In a family holding such values, attitudes such as the superiority of men often prevail and a patriarchal hierarchy develops in which the father makes all the decisions, requires absolute obedience and controls the family's resources. Such values feed through into a world where 'might is right', where the strong prevail and the weak, the ill, the disabled, the poor, the minorities only exist to provide the labour and consume the goods and services of the factories and businesses of the rich and powerful. On the world stage, these attitudes and values produce a global order in which strong countries dictate the terms of trade and the world financial framework in such a way that poorer countries remain poor. These attitudes result in businesses that are ruthlessly competitive regardless of the cost in human or environmental terms, in governments whose sole aim is to remain in power rather than to serve their people, in institutions that appear to be more interested in expanding their role and fulfilling management targets than in serving the public. They result in nations and social groups dominating and tyrannising other nations and social groups, producing frustration, resentment, rebellion and even terrorism. They mean that women will always be at a disadvantage in such societies, which are consequently patriarchal, male-dominated and hierarchical. Ultimately, they produce an environment in which oppression of minority groups and the disadvantaged, and even domestic violence, is justified. Far from creating a stable community, such hierarchical societies – and families – are very volatile, as they are based on unnatural, unjust relationships against which people chafe and rebel. Thus, implicit in any hierarchy is compulsion, force, if necessary even violence to maintain the structure.

Because these hierarchical structures are so deeply ingrained in our patterns of thought, they appear part of reality itself and people are even afraid of the anarchy that might result if they abandoned them. It is argued that it is part of human nature for one set of human beings to seek to dominate others, for war to occur and for extremes of wealth and poverty to exist. Part of the reason for the paralysis of will to change anything comes from this inability to see an alternative. But it also partly comes from the fact that, during the last hundred years, many movements have arisen that have promised to revolutionise human society and yet have basically changed nothing. The various communist revolutions, for example, promised a new, fairer, more egalitarian order but ended up with societies that were just as hierarchical and just as oppressive to those at the bottom of the hierarchy as the regimes they replaced. But another part of the reason for the lack of any movement is the very subversive nature of power itself. How can one overcome a powerful government except by becoming more powerful? Thus, power as a value always remains at the centre of society whatever the identity of the holder of that power. And the destructive, negative effects described above are thus inevitable and inherent aspects of these hierarchical societies.

Among the most radical of the Baha'i teachings is the framework for a new type of society proposed by Baha'u'llah, one that is not based on power and is not hierarchical. Starting with the overarching concept of unity that envelops all aspects of the Baha'i Faith, Baha'u'llah states that one aspect of this unity is that all people should see themselves as equal to others, and no one should exalt himself or herself over anyone else. The analogy that is made in the Baha'i scriptures is that of an organism. An animal has different organs but all of them are necessary and important for the proper functioning of the organism. The liver is as important as the heart or the kidneys or the skin. Even the brain cannot function without the kidneys or the lungs. They are all interconnected and interdependent and all are important; there is an overarching unity of function that enables a living organism to exist. This is the analogy for society. No part of it or individual member of it is more important than any other.

This non-hierarchical social framework operates for Baha'is at all levels. Thus, within the family, the equality of women and men is emphasised and decision-making through consultation is encouraged. Within the Baha'i community itself there is no individual leadership. Leadership and authority rest with elected institutions when they are acting as institutions and the individuals who are elected onto them have no personal rank or authority. Decisions are made through consultative processes that are designed to ensure that every member of the community – women, members of minority groups, young people, the poor and all of those who do not get heard in our present society – have an input into the process.

Indeed, in the Baha'i Faith some words associated with the push towards competitiveness, which is so characteristic of hierarchical societies, are defined in such a way as to subvert their current meanings. Thus, for example, 'Abdu'l-Baha writes that, for the Baha'i cause, 'victory' is 'to submit and yield' ('Abdu'l-Bahá, 1978, p. 256) and he quotes Baha'u'llah as stating: 'Therefore, today, "victory" neither hath been, nor will be opposition to anyone, nor strife with any person; but rather what is well-pleasing – this is, that the cities of men's hearts, which are under the dominion of the hosts of selfishness and lust, should be subdued by the sword of the Word of Wisdom, and of Exhortation' (Bahá'u'lláh, quoted in 'Abdu'l-Baha, 1891, p. 114). Similarly, 'Abdu-'l -Baha changes the concept of competition from its usual role in a masculine, hierarchical society – that of gaining power – and instead promotes it as an approach in the arena of service: 'Vie ye with each other in the service of God and of His Cause. This is indeed what profiteth you in this world, and in that which is to come' ('Abdu'l-Bahá, quoted in Shoghi Effendi, 1990, p. 83). The goal of personal ambition and the source of greatest glory do not belong, in 'Abdu'l-Baha's estimation, to the person who seizes power but to the person who excels in service to 'human uplift and betterment' ('Abdu'l-Bahá, 1982, p. 353) and to 'the cause of the Most Great Peace' (ibid. p. 123).

Baha'is therefore work from the premise that were this non-hierarchical structure to society to be realised, a great number of the problems facing the world would be resolved; among them the violence of war caused by the desire by one country to dominate another; the unfair terms of trade and financial arrangement imposed upon the poor countries by the rich; the resentment and bitterness caused by the domination of one group over another, resulting in frustration, violence and terrorism; the pollution and poor working environments created by the drive to compete and to succeed at all costs. It would also be a major advance towards some of the other main Baha'i teachings: creating equality between women and men; freeing society of the many prejudices that hold down many groups in society; and reducing poverty in society.

This understanding of the basic changes required in society and the values that underpin them informs the Baha'i attitudes towards many of the social issues confronting humanity. For example, it is clear that a society that is based on the understanding of the equality of all people will be free of racism, sexism, xenophobia, class prejudice, religious bigotry, nationalism and all the other manifestations of intolerance that stem from failing to acknowledge the oneness of humanity. At the same time, Baha'is appreciate that the world in which we live has not yet made these structural changes and it is therefore vital that work is done now to address specific issues. In other words, simultaneous with developing the spiritual values that will effect such changes and with spreading the Baha'i teachings, so that significant numbers of people adopt them and lend their weight to the changes required, it is important to work with other social agencies and governments to make the gradual changes that lead in this general direction. Thus, at the global level, Baha'is work in partnership with institutions such as the United Nations and its agencies to develop practical measures to combat racism and they lobby to ensure that such measures include an understanding of the spiritual and moral values required for the steps taken to be effective. At the local level, Baha'is cooperate with other non-governmental organisations, interfaith groups, women's organisations and so on that are working on such issues and they participate in local initiatives such as Local Agenda 21 and race equality forums that promote and execute programmes designed to change social attitudes and structures. In addition, Baha'is offer their communities as models of how social change can be effected. For example, the principles of the oneness of humanity and the abandonment of prejudice are demonstrated within the Baha'i community by the large number of marriages across ethnic, cultural, racial, national and religious heritages; while consultation is advanced as a decision-making tool for families, government and businesses alike.

Recognising that social issues are interconnected and that progress on all of them must begin somewhere, Baha'i efforts are at present focused on four general, overlapping areas: human rights, the status of women, the prosperity of humankind and moral development.

Human Rights

The Baha'i position on human rights was outlined as long ago as February 1947 when the Baha'i International Community presented 'A Baha'i Declaration of Human Obligations and Rights' to the first session of the United Nations Commission on Human Rights in Lake Success, New York: 'The source of human rights is the endowment of qualities, virtues and powers which God has bestowed upon mankind without discrimination of sex, race, creed or nation. To fulfil the possibilities of this divine endowment is the purpose of human existence.' However, the realisation of these rights depends on a social framework with a legitimate government at its head. Thus, 'a human right is an expression of man's divine endowment given social status by a moral and sovereign body' (Bahá'í International Community, 1947).

Baha'is recognise that the full establishment and exercise of human rights involves not only government action and international legislation but also requires the building of the new sort of social order outlined above. Moreover, human rights are ultimately based on the recognition by ordinary people of the reality of human unity. For individuals, this comes down to accepting responsibility for upholding the rights of other members of the community.

Popularly, human rights are often equated with social justice alone, that is, with the extension to underprivileged individuals and groups of the benefits of social, political and economic welfare enjoyed by other sections of society. For Baha'is, however, human rights are more basic even than this and an extensive range of interrelated human rights is alluded to in the Baha'i teachings. The most fundamental of these is the right of each individual to investigate reality for himself. Underpinning this is the belief that all individuals have the capacity to undertake such an investigation. For people to exercise this right, they must have education; thus the right of all children to an education is embedded in the Baha'i teachings, as is the right of access to information. A corollary to the right to investigate reality for oneself is freedom of thought and its parallel, freedom of belief, from which springs the right to worship as one chooses. Freedom of speech and freedom of movement are linked to these rights.

For Baha'is, 'rights' are not synonymous with licence. For example, the right of the individual to freedom of action does not imply the fanatical pursuit of individualism that undermines social responsibility and jeopardises the welfare of others. Similarly, freedom of speech and thought includes the understanding that individuals will express these appropriately. While the enjoyment of individual human rights does not mean that every social benefit is to be bestowed on a person by the community or the government without cost, individuals should be able to rely on their communities and governments to provide an environment in which they can live safely and exercise their rights and privileges in a responsible way.

> Since the body of humankind is one and indivisible, each
> member of the race is born into the world as a trust of the whole.
> This trusteeship constitutes the moral foundation of most of the
> other rights – principally economic and social – which the instru-
> ments of the United Nations are attempting similarly to define.
> The security of the family and the home, the ownership of prop-
> erty, and the right to privacy are all implied in such a trusteeship.
> The obligations on the part of the community extend to the
> provision of employment, mental and physical health care, social
> security, fair wages, rest and recreation, and a host of other
> reasonable expectations on the part of the individual members
> of society. (Bahá'í International Community, 1995a)

Baha'is recognise that one of the main obstacles to safeguarding
human rights is the widely held conviction of some national governments that the exercise of their sovereignty permits them to withhold
such rights from some or all of their citizens. For Baha'is, such a posture
lends even greater urgency to the need to establish the foundations of a
world federal government that can, among other functions, oversee the
extension of human rights to all people.

As for the practical steps being taken, individual Baha'is and
Baha'i communities locally, nationally and internationally are actively
engaged in such undertakings as human rights education, anti-racism
programmes, interfaith dialogue and activities that foster the advancement of women. In addition, the behaviour of individual Baha'is, their
practice within their own families and the very working of the worldwide Baha'i community itself are practical ways in which Baha'is
demonstrate their awareness of human rights and are working to
implement them.

The Status of Women

> Dignity before God depends, not on sex, but on purity and
> luminosity of heart. Human virtues belong equally to all!
> ('Abdu'l-Bahá, 1967, p. 162)

> The world of humanity has two wings – one is women and the
> other men. Not until both wings are equally developed can
> the bird fly. Should one wing remain weak, flight is impossi-
> ble. Not until the world of women becomes equal to the
> world of men in the acquisition of virtues and perfections, can
> success and prosperity be attained as they ought to be.
> ('Abdu'l-Bahá, 1978, p. 302)

Not only are women to be extended human rights but a key component
of the prosperity of humanity is the advancement of women. Further,

> The emancipation of women, the achievement of full equality between the sexes, is one of the most important, though less acknowledged prerequisites of peace. The denial of such equality perpetrates an injustice against one half of the world's population and promotes in men harmful attitudes and habits that are carried from the family to the workplace, to political life, and ultimately to international relations. There are no grounds, moral, practical, or biological, upon which such denial can be justified. Only as women are welcomed into full partnership in all fields of human endeavour will the moral and psychological climate be created in which international peace can emerge. (Universal House of Justice, 1985c, para. 33)

Baha'is believe that world peace itself is dependent on a profound understanding of the equality of women and men and the application of this knowledge to all social transactions.

The role of women in establishing world peace was particularly emphasised by 'Abdu'l-Baha in his addresses while travelling in North America in 1912. At that time, American women were seeking the vote and 'Abdu'l-Baha linked women's suffrage to securing international peace, stating that 'universal peace is impossible without universal suffrage' ('Abdu'l-Bahá, 1982, p. 134). 'So it will come to pass,' he declared, 'that when women participate fully and equally in the affairs of the world, when they enter confidently and capably the great arena of laws and politics, war will cease; for woman will be the obstacle and hindrance to it' (ibid. p. 135). Thus Baha'is expect women to undertake civic responsibilities as well as ones centring on the home.

In the first instance, it is the home that is to provide the values, attitudes, behaviours and practices that will enable girls and women to shoulder responsibilities both within the home and without. The dignity afforded to women and their equal treatment are basic to their empowerment, while their participation in consultation within the home setting provides a skill that is transferable to the workplace and the political arena. The Baha'i community provides further opportunities for women to advance and to use their capacities, for example as decision-makers within the elected administrative bodies on which they serve, as advisers on the appointed bodies and as training institute tutors and teachers of the Baha'i Faith to others.

Baha'is consider women to have a primary role in many of the functions and activities of society and expect them to be key players in such areas as arts and sciences (ibid. p. 283), particularly the industrial and agricultural sciences, education, health and health promotion. For example, owing to their role as the primary carers of children, the elderly and the infirm, not only are women central to maintaining the health of their own families, but in many communities around the world their knowledge is indispensable for securing the health of the wider society. However, because women are marginalised in many societies, or confined to their homes, their wisdom and skills are seldom acknowledged and they are generally not asked to participate in the decision-making that shapes policy in these areas.

Baha'is seek to reverse this and to raise the status of women so that their insights and skills are available to the wider community and to provide them with the opportunities for their own advancement. Thus to enable women to take on a wider range of tasks and to ensure that they are discharged in a responsible way, Baha'is urge governments to give the highest attention to the education of girls and women. Baha'is themselves give priority to the education of girls over boys when they cannot educate all their children. Baha'is recognise that education and vocational and professional training must be organised in such a way that more girls and women can take advantage of them. Several Baha'i development projects focus on empowering women as educators, primary care health workers and nutritionists. For example, they have established a model training programme for volunteer community health workers which is being adapted for use around the world. Baha'i-inspired organisations, such as the European Baha'i Business Forum, promote the partnership of women and men in the workplace and run programmes that enable women to become entrepreneurs.

At the international level, Baha'is have long participated in United Nations summits and conferences on the status of women and made significant representations to their deliberations. In addition, at UN conferences that focus on other subjects, such as human rights, health or social development, Baha'is draw particular attention in their submissions to the roles and needs of women. In particular, Baha'is have made significant contributions to deliberations concerning the education of girls, consistently pointing out that 'Not only must girl children receive adequate food, health care, and education, they must be given every opportunity to develop their capacities. As women become educated and enter all fields of human endeavour, they will make unique contributions to the creation of a just world order' (Bahá'í International Community, 1992).

The Prosperity of Humankind

The challenges facing humanity are complex and interrelated. Baha'is do not underestimate the collective and individual effort that will be required if these are to be met effectively. Many of these challenges arise because the world community has, on the one hand, failed to achieve a lasting and universal peace and, on the other, lacks a recognition of the oneness of humanity that would enable that peace to be established. Thus, while Baha'is believe that 'world peace is not only possible but inevitable' (Universal House of Justice, 1985c, para. 1), Baha'u'llah also states: 'The well-being of mankind, its peace and security, are unattainable unless and until its unity is firmly established' (Bahá'u'lláh, 1983, p. 286).

Failure to address the issues facing humanity leads not only to obvious human tragedies, such as poverty, famine, disease and, ultimately, the untimely death of thousands if not millions of people, it also turns these into seedbeds for racism, social unrest and violence, terrorism and war, which further contribute to poverty, famine, disease and death. The cycle cannot be broken, Baha'is believe, by simply tackling each of these issues on their own, important and urgent as this is. Collective action, taken by a world federal government, will be required. However, recognising that work needs to be done in parallel with efforts to establish such a government, Baha'is strongly support programmes of social and economic development, poverty eradication, social cohesion, health promotion, education and welfare, and there are currently over 2,000 Baha'i-inspired projects and organisations dealing with these issues.

Baha'is recognise that poverty is one of the most complex problems facing humanity in the 21st century. The eradication of poverty is high on the agenda of the international community, yet efforts to deal with it effectively have not yet met with great success. This is due, Baha'is believe, to a failure to tackle the underlying problem of the world's disunity and an inability to channel resources to where they are needed most because the global political framework to do so does not yet exist. Further, both donors and recipients of aid have concerns about each other's ethics and probity and cases of corruption have blighted relationships and undermined confidence. It has become clear that 'aid', financial restructuring and even debt relief are short-term answers and sometimes even add to the problem rather than resolve it. Baha'is believe that working on a number of fronts simultaneously – including the education of women, developing moral leadership, work creation, the empowerment of young people and voluntary sharing, as well as efforts to establish a framework of global governance – is essential to addressing this thorny problem.

Another social issue that needs urgent attention is the environment. Environmental degradation, climate change and the unrestricted exploitation and depletion of the earth's resources are themes that engage the attention of many people, non-governmental organisations and businesses as well as governments and multi-state organisations, such as the United Nations and the European Union. People may worry about what is happening to the environment but feel powerless to do anything significant. While it is true that many environmental issues can only be tackled by governments, businesses and international organisations working in concert, Baha'is believe that individuals do bear some responsibility and have a significant role to play. It is individuals who can foster in themselves and in their families the spiritual values and insights found in the Baha'i scriptures that inform humanity's relationship with nature.

Baha'is are not sentimental about nature but believe it to be a reflection of God. Thus the Baha'i Faith espouses a reverence for all life and Baha'is hold nature in high regard. Baha'u'llah taught that nature in its essence is the embodiment of the name of God; it is 'God's Will and is its expression in and through the contingent world'. He encouraged his followers to 'Look at the world and ponder a while upon it', as doing so would enable the earth itself to 'acquaint' humans 'with that which is within it and upon it' and give them 'such clear explanations' as to make them 'independent of every eloquent expounder' (Bahá'u'lláh, 1988b, pp. 141–2). Thus, individuals can develop an understanding of the natural world as a unified system and cultivate a deep appreciation of the relationship between the environment and human beings. At a practical level, they can examine their own values and the lifestyles that emerge from them and determine where changes can be made. For example, they can take modest measures to recycle or compost their rubbish, use their cars less often or turn off unnecessary lights. They can change the value they place on material objects and physical comfort and convenience and alter their patterns of consumption. These may appear to be meagre efforts and too insignificant to deal effectively with overwhelming environmental problems, yet they demonstrate the relationship between values and action and illustrate the kinds of individual behaviour that will promote the development of a more sustainable society.

An allied social issue is agriculture and food production in general. These are linked not only to environmental concerns but also to health matters in several directions, ranging from the risk of pesticides and contaminants in food to unhealthy food choices leading to obesity, particularly in children. Many western countries have played down the importance of agriculture or have jeopardised the production of various crops, yet Baha'u'llah warned that 'Special regard must be paid to agriculture' (ibid. p. 90), asserting that it is 'conducive to the advancement of mankind and to the reconstruction of the world' (ibid. p. 89). 'Abdu'l-Baha called agriculture and 'tillage of the soil' the 'fundamental basis of the community' ('Abdu'l-Bahá, 1982, p. 217) and outlined how a village storehouse and its urban equivalent should function (see 'Abdu'l-Baha, 1945, pp. 39–41). Thus, at the global level, Baha'is support UN strategies to enhance agricultural development and to increase food security; for example, the Baha'i International Community is the convenor of the 'Advocates for African Food Security: Lessening the Burden for Women', a coalition of non-governmental organisations. At the individual level, Baha'is are enjoined to 'lend their support' to agricultural development (Shoghi Effendi, 1926), while local spiritual assemblies are 'to promote the standards of agriculture and other skills in the life of the people' through consultation and the application of 'such Baha'i principles as harmony between science and religion, the importance of education, and work as a form of worship' (Universal House of Justice, 1976).

A related issue is animal rights. Compassion for animals is a fundamental tenet of the Baha'i Faith. Baha'is are to 'show forth the utmost loving-kindness to every living creature', 'the more the better', and because animals are unable to protest the cruelty done to them, 'Abdu'l-Baha stated: 'Therefore is it essential that ye show forth the utmost consideration to the animal, and that ye be even kinder to him than to your fellow-man' ('Abdu'l-Bahá, 1978, pp. 158–9). Part of the education of children should be the proper treatment of animals.

> Train your children from their earliest days to be infinitely tender and loving to animals. If an animal be sick, let the children try to heal it, if it be hungry, let them feed it, if thirsty, let them quench its thirst, if weary, let them see that it rests.
> ('Abdu'l-Bahá, 1978, p. 159)

Baha'is are allowed to hunt for food but 'not to excess' (Bahá'u'lláh, 1992, para. 60) and it is anticipated that in the future people will be vegetarians. Regarding using animals for research, 'Abdu'l-Baha, in a letter stressing the need for kindness to animals, indicated that it would be 'permissible to perform an operation on a living animal for the purposes of research even if the animal were killed thereby, but that animal must be well anaesthetised and that the utmost care must be exercised that it does not suffer' (Universal House of Justice, 1978). Beyond this, it is at present left to the conscience of individuals to make decisions on this subject in light of the general Baha'i teachings on animal welfare (the Universal House of Justice may legislate in future on ethical issues that are not specifically mentioned in the Baha'i writings).

Such considerations must also be seen in the light of the Baha'i teachings on health and healing, access to health care, medicine and medical ethics, all major issues confronting humanity today. The Baha'i teachings on health are intertwined with the Baha'i view of the essentially spiritual nature of human beings. Thus, Baha'is understand that health is more than merely the absence of disease and recognise that it has not only physical, mental and social aspects but a spiritual dimension as well. The body is seen as the 'throne of the inner temple' (The Báb, 1976, p. 95) and it is to be kept healthy and is to be protected. This has implications not only for how one treats one's own body, in terms of nutrition, exercise and abstaining from drugs, alcohol and harmful and degrading practices, but also for the responsibility of government and social agencies to provide access to health and health promotion; it also informs the roles to be played by health professionals, communities and families, and women as the agents of primary health care involved in maintaining family and community health. Thus health is, on the one hand, an issue to be addressed by each level of society and, on the other, itself has an impact on each level.

Baha'is support UN efforts and the efforts of their own governments to secure access to health services and appropriate medicine for all people and many Baha'i communities and agencies provide health-related services as social development projects. Many of these projects focus on education, particularly the education of women as the front-line deliverers of nutrition, healthy living practices and health care to their families and communities. Further, they aim to move ordinary people, particularly women, from the fringes of policy-making about health matters to the centre by providing skills such as consultation that will enable people to engage in decision-making about an issue that affects their own lives so profoundly. At the same time, Baha'is recognise that the ability of governments to provide adequate health services hinges very much on the wider issues surrounding poverty and development, which can best be addressed by an integrated approach at the global level and, ultimately, by a world government.

Among the health issues on which Baha'is have made representations to their governments or to the United Nations are female genital mutilation and HIV/AIDS, both of which Baha'is identify as complex issues arising, at least in part, from persistent gender inequality and culturally accepted social inequalities. Solutions to both are correspondingly complex as well as elusive. Baha'is actively work with other organisations and agencies to promote the discontinuance of the practice of female circumcision and they recognise that medical advances and access to appropriate medicines are necessary to the control and eventual eradication of HIV/AIDS. While immediate practical steps need to be taken to curtail both, long-term solutions must also be effected, particularly education that will change attitudes and will lead towards more responsible sexual behaviour. Baha'is accept that, ultimately, 'nothing short of a spiritual transformation will move men – and women – to forego the behaviours' that contribute to the continuance and spread of HIV/AIDS (Bahá'í International Community, 2001a). At the same time, Baha'is have called upon religious leaders and all people of faith to respond with compassion to those affected by the HIV/AIDS pandemic and to show true moral leadership by ridding themselves of judgemental attitudes and providing an environment of love and understanding.

In recent years, scientific advances have spawned a host of ethical issues that have gained media prominence and have challenged individuals and their governments, including the irradiation and genetic modification of food, genetic engineering, genetic screening, cloning, stem cell research and euthanasia. Baha'is acknowledge that these issues, and others, are complex and believe that 'an informed opinion can be offered only when the scientific understanding is much further advanced than at present and the social implications are clearer'. Baha'is are, therefore, 'free to come to their own conclusions based on their knowledge of the Baha'i teachings on nature and the purpose of life'. Furthermore, they are urged not to make dogmatic statements on such matters or to present their own ideas as the teachings of the Baha'i Faith (Universal House of Justice, 1997).

At the same time, Baha'is are well aware of the moral dangers and health risks arising from substance abuse and the trafficking and criminality that this engenders. People of all ages and from all backgrounds subject themselves to the harmful effects of drugs and alcohol for a variety of reasons, ranging from pleasure and recreation to curiosity and a way of dealing with stress and personal sorrow. Drug and alcohol abuse has increased significantly in recent years and has reached epidemic proportions in some parts of the world, affecting adolescents and children – the most vulnerable targets for dealers. Baha'is believe families, schools, religious organisations, the media and communities are front-line defences against increased substance use. They should set good examples and provide models of behaviour and an education that enables people to develop a spiritual orientation, which would assist them to develop positive attitudes towards themselves, others and their environment. At the same time Baha'is believe that government and enforcement agencies should step up their work to reduce drug supply and provide avenues for addicts and abusers to treat their dependency. At the international level, governments should work together to curb the production and traffic in drugs. Baha'i families and communities are striving to address this issue, through educational programmes that foster the development of moral and spiritual attitudes and behaviours and by setting an example by themselves abstaining from the use of alcohol and drugs.

Baha'is take a similar approach to human trafficking. In his Most Holy Book, the Kitab-i-Aqdas, Baha'u'llah prohibited slavery (Bahá-'u'lláh, 1992, para. 72) and in a letter written to Queen Victoria commended her for forbidding 'the trading in slaves, both men and women' (quoted in Shoghi Effendi, 1980, p. 35). Trafficking in women for prostitution – a perilous and gross injustice to women and a blatant manifestation of inequality – is wholly condemned. Baha'is urge governments and international bodies to legislate against trafficking, to take vigorous action against traffickers and to provide adequate protection to the victims of trafficking.

At the same time, civil war, religious and political persecution, famine and poverty have vastly increased the number of refugees and asylum seekers. Countries around the world struggle to cope with the influx of huge numbers of people who are compelled to leave their own homes to seek safety, food, shelter or simply a better life. Such a situation not only places huge burdens on the host population but also tears the fabric of society, destroys families and degrades the human spirit of those forced to leave their homes. Baha'is anticipated such forced migration would be one outcome of the historical unwillingness of governments to improve their own internal governance, on the one hand, and to find effective ways of working together at the international level, on the other. Baha'is believe it is now urgent that governments not only address the immediate needs of asylum seekers but also the underlying causes.

The effects of globalisation on communities around the world are marked and the positive outcomes of the process often appear to be outweighed by the negative, leading to deepening poverty rather than prosperity. Baha'is understand globalisation to be the inevitable outcome of the impulse towards world unity and peace initiated by the coming of Baha'u'llah and his teaching regarding the elimination of the extremes of wealth and poverty as the foundation of a prosperous world economy. They recognise that the most effective way to control the direction of globalisation is through good governance at the international level. From a Baha'i perspective, nations, social groups, individuals and businesses need to operate within a global framework that curbs any tendencies to draw undue power, wealth or resources to themselves and protects others within the system from exploitation. A key element of this process is the responsibility of business to act ethically and in the wider interests of humanity. Baha'is acknowledge the ability of the business community to generate wealth and subsequently prosperity, but they believe that its potential must be harnessed for the good of humanity and not merely for one sector; moreover, business should not be beyond the reach of legal and moral constraints. Baha'is actively promote the development of a world economy, controlled by a world federal government working in the best interests of all people and nations, and the creation of a single world currency.

Underpinning every functioning society is a system of justice and its legal and law enforcement framework and these in turn are based on the notions of justice and the values the society holds regarding the sanctity of life and the protection of the individual and property. Baha'is believe justice systems should be rooted in an appreciation of the spiritual nature of the human being and an understanding of how people respond to reward and punishment. Baha'is are strong supporters of the rule of law and they obey and are loyal to the governments under which they live. Justice is the principal social value brought by Baha'u'llah and on it hinges the establishment of social order and the unity of humanity (see Baha'u'llah, 1988b, pp. 66–7). It is the responsibility of society at all levels to develop just laws that protect the rights of individuals and communities, especially minorities, and to punish offenders. Thus one of the institutions of the world federal government envisaged by Baha'is is an international tribunal and the Baha'i community championed the establishment of the International Criminal Court in the Hague.

It is important, Baha'is believe, to address these issues from all directions, from the grassroots up and from the top down, individually and as part of an integrated programme. Failure to do so not only exacerbates the ill effects of the individual problem but such effects are compounded across the whole of society. As it was the purpose of Baha'u'llah to bring unity to the world at all levels, from the family to the globe, Baha'is applaud every effort to create social cohesion and prosperity for the greatest numbers and to prevent disunity, which too often results in social unrest, rioting and, ultimately, war.

This brief look at some of the social issues addressed by the Baha'i teachings cannot be divorced from the Baha'i understanding of the essentially spiritual nature of human beings, their concept of the kinds of communities and social structures that are best suited to people's needs and their beliefs about the values, attitudes, behaviours and practices that will achieve this.

Moral Development

> Religion is the greatest of all means for the establishment of
> order in the world and for the peaceful contentment of all that
> dwell therein. (Bahá'u'lláh, cited in Shoghi Effendi, 1991, p. 186)

Baha'is see the decline of religion as a social force as being the chief
cause of the 'perversion of human nature, the degradation of human
conduct, the corruption and dissolution of human institutions' (Shoghi
Effendi, 1991, p. 187), resulting in many of the ills and dangers
presently facing society, from anti-social behaviour to terrorism, from
religious intolerance and racial hatred to fraud and crime. Baha'is
believe that some of the social phenomena seen today are abnormalities
of human nature caused by the current distortion of the social
environment owing to a lack of spiritual values and that these will tend
to be resolved when the social environment is improved and spiritual
values are restored. Thus Baha'is assert that it is vital to reclaim the
religious values that will both protect and promote the welfare of
individuals and their communities. They see that it is essential to win
the support of the generality of mankind for the standards of human
conduct that derive from a profound appreciation and application of
spiritual principles.

By 'spiritual' they do not mean vague ideas and pious or sentimental
hopes, adherence to which, it is expected, will banish all ills. Rather the
term refers to that cluster of practical virtues and values born out of a
vision and understanding of God's purpose for humanity that underpins our relationships with each other at every level – personal, family,
community, national and global. Some of these virtues can be identified
as absolutely imperative for the smooth running of any social unit,
whether it be the family or the world: justice, trustworthiness, honesty,
courtesy, patience, love, selflessness, etc. These virtues – or lack of
them – form the basis of our value system which in turn shapes our attitudes and determines our behaviour and practice. Because human
beings are fundamentally spiritual, it is only in societies that prioritise
the moral, ethical, emotional and intellectual development of the individual that people are likely to become service-oriented members of
society who contribute constructively to the community and put the
interests of others before their own.

Responsibility for creating and maintaining a moral environment
devolves on families, communities and government. The Baha'i writings mention three sorts of education: material – concerned with the
development of the body; human – knowledge of arts and sciences;

and spiritual – concerning the development of character and the acquisition of values. Education of children at home and in schools must be focused on all three, ensuring an appreciation of the oneness of humanity, on the one hand, and the acquisition and implementation of virtues, on the other. Together these provide the vision, values, behaviours and skills that enable young people to resist harmful habits such as drug abuse, to reject attitudes such as racism and prejudice, and to lend their weight to endeavours that promote safer, healthier and more united communities. At the same time, moral education will help young people realise that they are members of a single, worldwide human family in which they have both rights and responsibilities and where they are expected to respect the rights of others. To advance this principle, over the years Baha'is have developed moral education classes that are open to all children.

Thus Baha'is believe that the development of sustainable communities and material progress hinge on the application of spiritual, or moral, values and must reflect spiritual principles and priorities. In this connection, of all the virtues that people are to acquire 'Abdu'l-Baha identified trustworthiness as the primary one.

> . . . in the sight of God, trustworthiness is the bedrock of His Faith and the foundation of all virtues and perfections. A man deprived of this quality is destitute of everything. What shall faith and piety avail if trustworthiness be lacking? Of what consequence can they be? What benefit or advantage can they confer? *('Abdu'l-Bahá, in Compilation, 1991, vol. 2, p. 340)*

Lack of trustworthiness distorts human relationships, fosters suspicion and frustrates simple human transactions. In its extreme form – corruption – lack of trustworthiness undermines the ability of leadership at any level to function properly and promulgates injustices. Thus Baha'is commend the cultivation of trustworthiness in the individual, in families and communities and, particularly, in those who hold positions of authority and responsibility – government, public servants, business and leaders at all levels. Further, for Baha'is, moral leadership at any level – whether of parents in the family or in national government – is to be founded on an attitude of service to others.

> Service to humanity is service to God. *('Abdu'l-Bahá, 1982, p. 8)*

Moral leadership, the leadership of the future, will find its highest expression in service to others and to the community as a whole. It will foster collective decision-making and collective action and will be motivated by a commitment to justice, including the equality of women and men, and to the well-being of all humanity. Moral leadership will manifest itself in adherence to a single standard of conduct in both public and private life, for leaders and for citizens alike. *(Bahá'í International Community, 1998)*

This is closely allied with the Baha'i attitude towards work: 'Work done in the spirit of service is the highest form of worship' ('Abdu'l-Bahá, in *Compilation*, 1991, vol. 1, p. 313).

At the international level, Baha'is are heartened by UN action plans that acknowledge the spiritual dimension of human beings and its significance to the welfare of the planet. For example, the Copenhagen Declaration arising from the 1995 Summit on Social Development asserted 'our societies must respond more effectively to the material and spiritual needs of individuals, their families and the communities in which they live . . . not only as a matter of urgency but also as a matter of sustained and unshakeable commitment through the years ahead' (Copenhagen Declaration, 1995). In the preamble to the Habitat Agenda, the product of the Second World Summit on Human Settlements in 1996, the world's governments committed themselves to 'achieving a world of greater stability and peace, built on ethical and spiritual vision' (Habitat Agenda, 1996). Such proclamations mark significant progress in global thinking and Baha'is await the policies and actions that will turn such sentiments into practical outcomes.

***

For Baha'is, progress in every area mentioned above is dependent on knowledge, volition and action. Without knowledge, efforts to change people and societies are misdirected, at best ineffective and at worst harmful. Without individual, social and political will, such concepts are nothing but utopian ideals and interesting talking points. Without purposeful action, good intentions are just blueprints on a shelf. Individual values, attitudes, behaviours and practices are intimately connected to their expression in society at every level. Changing society at every level is, for Baha'is, dependent on the implementation of spiritual values and priorities.

We need a change of heart, a reframing of all our conceptions and a new orientation of our activities. The inward life of man as well as his outward environment have to be reshaped if human salvation is to be secured. (Shoghi Effendi, 1932)

The Baha'i International Community

It is the responsibility of individual Baha'is, local communities and spiritual assemblies at both local and national levels to advocate and work for the realisation of the principles outlined above. At the international level, the Baha'i International Community (BIC) undertakes these tasks on behalf of the worldwide Baha'i community. The Baha'i International Community was established in 1948 by Shoghi Effendi as an international non-governmental organisation registered with the United Nations Office of Public Information. Today it is the organisation through which the Universal House of Justice interfaces with all international organisations.

From the beginning, the Baha'i Faith has advocated the development of international organisations and has established relationships with them as they have been created. Baha'u'llah himself called for the world's leaders to convoke international summits to discuss the establishment of world peace and to conclude treaties to ensure it (Bahá'u'lláh, 1988a, pp. 30–1), while 'Abdu'l-Baha laid out the agenda for such summits and urged the formation of a permanent international organisation to uphold peace and provide a framework for the execution of the rule of law at the global level.

When the League of Nations was established, 'Abdu'l-Baha applauded its creation while noting its inadequacies. An International Baha'i Bureau was established in Geneva, the seat of the League of Nations, in 1926 to foster a relationship with the League and to provide a meeting place for Baha'is attending its sessions. Baha'is were particularly active in the discussions of the League on disarmament. In 1928 the Baha'is of Iraq brought an appeal to the League to protect the House of Baha'u'llah in Baghdad. While a decision was made in favour of the Baha'is, it was never carried out. The International Baha'i Bureau remained open even after the League of Nations failed.

When the United Nations was established, Shoghi Effendi encouraged Baha'is worldwide to support it and its activities and many Baha'is did so by forming or joining United Nations Associations in their communities. When the UN Charter was drafted in San Francisco in 1945, the National Spiritual Assembly of the Baha'is of the United States and Canada sent two official observers to the event and later registered itself officially for observer status. In 1947 the UN Special Committee on Palestine asked Shoghi Effendi for the Baha'i opinion on the future of Palestine. In his response Shoghi Effendi expressed the desire of the Baha'i community for universal peace and justice and for reconciliation between Jews and Muslims, but he also underscored the non-political character of the Baha'i Faith.

In 1947 the BIC began its advocacy of human rights by presenting a statement to the UN on human obligations and rights, later endorsing the Genocide Convention. Over the years the BIC has continued to set out the Baha'i position on human rights in concept and position papers. When the human rights of Baha'is in Iran (1955) and Morocco (1962) were threatened, the BIC took steps to bring these to the attention of the UN. Latterly, the BIC has highlighted the plight of the Baha'is of Iran who since 1979 have suffered persecution at the hands of their government.

In 1955 the BIC set out its proposals for the revision of the UN charter, which were rewritten in 1995 for the 50th anniversary of the founding of the UN (see Baha'i International Community, 1995b). In 1967 the BIC set up a permanent office in New York and in 1970 it was granted consultative status (Category II) with the United Nations Economic and Social Council (ECOSOC). This enabled the BIC to present its views at formal sessions of ECOSOC's agencies. In 1976 the United Nations Children's Fund (UNICEF) also granted the BIC consultative status. In 1989 the BIC established working relations with the World Health Organisation (WHO).

From 1970 onwards, the BIC has brought before sessions of the UN and its agencies the Baha'i position on a wide range of issues and subjects addressed in the Baha'i teachings. It has particularly concentrated on the four thematic areas of human rights, the status of women, the prosperity of humankind and moral development, as well as on related topics such as social development, the family, youth and children, disabled people, the aged, population, human settlements, the environment, renewable energy sources, agriculture, science and technology, the law of the sea, crime prevention, drugs, disarmament and the peaceful uses of outer space.

From its inception, the Baha'i International Community has been one of the most active of the consultative NGOs within the UN system and is much respected by government and other NGOs alike. Today it is represented not only at the local level but also regionally and has offices in Geneva and Paris. Specialised offices in New York dedicated to the environment and the advancement of women ensure a focused approach to these issues.

Science and Religion

A central teaching of Baha'u'llah that underpins the thinking of Baha'is on social and development issues is that science and religion are different aspects of the same truth. In the modern world, people have become used to thinking of science and religion as two opposing areas of human life. This stems from the time when the Church was persecuting Galileo or opposing Darwin's theory of evolution. Owing to the success of science in describing reality and in creating the technologies that have transformed the world, people have tended to discard religion as a tool for creating social policy and interacting with the world and have assumed that science would provide all the answers to humanity's problems.

As humanity moved into the 20th century, however, two things became clear. The first was that science itself is not as exact as had at first been thought. Starting with the Heisenberg Uncertainty Principle and becoming more obvious with Gödel's Theorem and chaos theory, it became clear that the original 18th- and 19th-century project of developing science until it explained everything was an impossibility. Science was capable of creating very exact knowledge but only about a circumscribed part of reality, never about the whole of reality. Thus science is complementary to religion, which does the opposite. Religion creates knowledge about the whole of reality but knowledge that is not very exact. The teachings of the founders of the world's religions each constitute, according to the teachings of Baha'u'llah, a complete, albeit highly metaphorical and non-linear, description of reality (see Hatcher, 2002, pp. 9–12). The second thing that became clear, and which is the result of the first, is that as one moves from the 'hard' physical sciences to the 'soft' human sciences, the explanatory and predictive power of science decreases. In physics, scientific formulas are explanatory and highly accurate in the predictions they make. In psychology and sociology, despite over a century of work, science only offers poor explanations and very inaccurate predictions. This is the equivalent of saying that as we move from the material world to the human world (which, according to the Baha'i teachings about the nature of the human being, is partly material and partly spiritual), the explanatory and predictive powers of science decrease. Baha'is believe, however, that as we move into this realm of the human world, the explanatory and predictive powers of religion increase. Religion is able to give us an accurate, although not a mathematical, linear, description of reality; it is capable of predicting that certain courses of action are likely to be productive and lead to beneficial results, while other courses of action will lead to destructive results.

If, as the Baha'i teachings suggest, human beings are both physical and spiritual in nature, then it stands to reason that any investigation, whether from the viewpoint of medicine, psychology, sociology, economics, urban planning or any other perspective, that looks only at the material and physical aspects of the human being, will look at only part of the picture and will not be as useful as an analysis that takes the spiritual aspect into account.

Religion and science are the two wings upon which man's intelligence can soar into the heights, with which the human soul can progress. It is not possible to fly with one wing alone! Should a man try to fly with the wing of religion alone he would quickly fall into the quagmire of superstition, whilst on the other hand, with the wing of science alone he would also make no progress, but fall into the despairing slough of materialism. All religions of the present day have fallen into superstitious practices, out of harmony alike with the true principles of the teaching they represent and with the scientific discoveries of the time . . . Much of the discord and disunion of the world is created by these man-made oppositions and contradictions. If religion were in harmony with science and they walked together, much of the hatred and bitterness now bringing misery to the human race would be at an end. *('Abdu'l-Bahá, 1967, pp. 143–4)*

In all then, the Baha'i teachings see science and religion as complementary. Each looks at a part of reality and in order to gain a profound understanding of reality, human beings need to engage with both. Both are valid sources of knowledge about reality. Science gives one sort of knowledge; knowledge that is exact, specific and clear about observable entities; it moves from the specific to the general and comprehensive, without ever managing to reach it. Religion gives knowledge that is non-linear and about abstract principles; knowledge that creates a comprehensive vision of reality but is non-specific about the detailed application of this knowledge.

But the Baha'i teachings go beyond just asserting that science and religion are complementary. They also assert that science and religion need each other. Religion needs science if it is to avoid becoming mired down in superstition. Science needs religion to guide it so that it does not become a source of evil in the world rather than a source of good. The Baha'i scriptures picture science and religion as the two wings on which the bird of humanity can fly upwards towards prosperity. Only if the two wings are equally strong and working in coordination can the bird reach its goal.

The Social Evolution of Humanity

Baha'is see the teachings that have been brought by Baha'u'llah as a culmination of the religious and social history of humanity. Human beings have evolved socially through ever greater stages of unity, through the stages of tribes, city-states and nations. This social evolution has been guided and brought about by the successive founders of the world's religions. Thus, these founders are seen as the guides of humanity in its development. The teaching that each of them has brought has been relevant to humanity's situation at the time that each came. Each of them has built on the teachings of his predecessor in the same way that the successive teachers that a child encounters at school build on what the previous teacher has taught. The fundamental reason for the presence in human history of the different religions of the world and their founders is the fact that humanity's requirements have changed.

Baha'u'llah claims to be the latest of these divine guides who has come with teachings that are relevant to humanity's current state of development. Humanity has evolved through its collective infancy, childhood and adolescence and has now reached, Baha'u'llah states, the stage of maturity. The hallmark of this maturity that humanity is just reaching is the realisation of the oneness of humanity, the arising of a global consciousness, and the appreciation of the interconnectedness of all life and of the physical and spiritual aspects of reality. The teachings that Baha'u'llah has brought all aim to give this spiritual unity, which has always existed, a physical shape in the form of human institutions that reflect the equality and unity of human beings and at the same time connect the physical and spiritual aspects of reality.

6

The Baha'i Vision of a United World

Baha'u'llah avowed that 'All men have been created to carry forward an ever-advancing civilization' (Bahá'u'lláh, 1983, p. 215). Baha'is believe that the sort of civilisation Baha'u'llah intended is not the materialistic, pleasure-oriented, unjust, poverty-ridden, cruel, war-torn, excessive society we now have. Of course, many elements of society are beautiful, cultured, useful, noble and worth carrying forward and it is true that in many ways life today is much better for great numbers than it was in the past. But it is also the case that the gap between rich and poor is widening, that in the process of globalisation many people are suffering, that while humanity seems to have reduced the possibility of all-out nuclear war, the world is faced with what appears to be an even more dreadful prospect – unnamed, undefined, fearless terrorism that makes murderers of children and ennobles suicide as long as it kills and maims others. Humanity seems to have lost sight of the civilising aspects of civilisation, the spiritual dimension to life that provides dignity to human beings and confers true joy.

The Baha'i Faith sets out the vision of a future united world commonwealth towards which humanity is striving and which inevitably will come about as a result of the application of the teachings and laws brought by Baha'u'llah. In such a world, peace will be permanently established, there will be universal prosperity and justice, the arts will flourish and a world civilisation will blossom. Despite appearances, Baha'is believe humanity is presently embarked on a course towards the political, social and spiritual unity that has been the vision of all religions and which up to now only the founders of the world's religions, poets and visionaries have described. Baha'is consider the evolution of such a mature world society to be not just desirable but imperative, not just possible but inevitable.

Such breathtaking claims are often criticised, ridiculed and dismissed by those who are not Baha'is as hopelessly utopian and optimistic, or even dangerous. Pointing to the warfare, hatred and divisiveness in the world, they ask how Baha'is can reconcile these facts with their assertions.

Baha'is point to the evolutionary nature of world progress, to the political and social developments of the last century and to the nature of the changes that are to come, changes which are at once social and spiritual and occur within society at large and within the individual. As at every other level of human relationship, from the family to the nation, at the global level Baha'is see a gradual but universal establishment of the ethical values, attitudes, behaviours and practices brought by Baha'u'llah.

The Social, Economic and Political Background

The Baha'i vision of the future is set against the political, economic, scientific and social developments of the late 19th and the 20th centuries. The Baha'i Faith emerged at time of tremendous social change, European expansionism and imperialism, and the industrialisation of the north. The first one hundred years of its existence coincide with the potato famine in Europe; the emigration of millions from Europe to North America; revolutions in Europe; the curtailment of the temporal power of the pope; the population explosion; the exploration of most parts of the world, including the poles; the scramble for Africa; a breakdown in the alliance system in Europe; two world wars; a revolution in communications and transportation; the rise of political movements both of the left and the right; the extension of the franchise, particularly to women; the creation of 'civil society'; the return of Jews to their spiritual homeland; the promulgation of major scientific theories such as evolution, the 'big bang' and relativity; huge advances in science and medicine (including the discovery of penicillin); changes in work patterns and the expansion of leisure activities; the extension of art to the broadcast media; the Great Depression and mass unemployment; the political empowerment of working people; and the creation of international institutions such as the League of Nations and the International Court of Arbitration. Then, as the Baha'i century turned in 1945, it coincided with the development and use of atomic weapons, the onset of the Cold War and the creation of the United Nations. In this period the political focus shifted from Europe to North America, the whole fabric of society changed and a triumvirate of social and economic theories, politics and science displaced religion. Change in the Cold War and post-Cold War era has been equally dramatic, with religion trying to make up for lost ground by re-emerging as fundamentalism, and terrorism becoming even more terrifying.

Baha'is see the political history of the world community as its attempt to develop ever more encompassing forms of government – beginning with the social unit of the family, through clan formation, tribal groupings, the development of nations and its corollary of the state, through attempts at state grouping in economic or quasi-political units. The final stage, according to the Baha'i writings, is a global grouping under a world government. Baha'is believe this is an inevitable step in the social evolution of the planet. They view the political history of the world over the past century as ever more successful attempts to establish this system. Therefore, to be brief and simplistic, the 19th-century alliance system broke down and produced the First World War. The resolution of this war saw early attempts to regulate international political affairs through the League of Nations. This blighted attempt itself broke down and was unequal to the task of preventing the Second World War. The outcome of that war saw a more vigorous attempt to establish some sort of universal political watchdog, in the form of the United Nations, an organisation with more 'teeth' than the League and to which more states could subscribe. The struggle of the world community of states to come to terms with the global nature of its concerns has not been yet wholly met by the United Nations, and it may be that this attempt, too, will fail, although Baha'is are strong supporters of its peacekeeping and development activities. This view of international political history by Baha'is gives them reason to believe that the establishment of a world government is inevitable.

Looking at this from a different perspective, the 20th century can also be understood as a period when religion was cast aside as inadequate and a series of ideologies was tried – ideologies that claimed to be 'scientific', because science was now the guarantor of truth in the place of religion, and claimed to be able to resolve the problems facing humanity, to give humanity a true picture of itself and a vision of what it should aim for collectively. These ideologies revolved around the three false gods identified by Shoghi Effendi: nationalism, racism and communism (Shoghi Effendi, 1980, p. 113). Hence, most of the history of the 20th century was tied up with the rise and fall of these ideologies and they have been seen to be the source of great human misery. In the West, for example, nationalism gave rise to the First World War that laid waste the continent of Europe and caused the western European powers to fall from their pre-eminent place among the nations of the world. The racist ideology of Nazi Germany exterminated millions of people and displaced millions more, produced the Second World War and caused even more widespread destruction in Europe and Asia, and, following the entry of Japan into the war, in the Pacific. The end of the 20th century witnessed the fall of communism, a completely materialistic ideology that put the state ahead of people and left behind a devastated landscape of ruined economies and polluted environments in Europe and Asia.

This history, from both perspectives, has given rise to a certain distrust of grand visions that claim to embrace the totality of human problems and situations. The world has settled into attempting to solve its problems in a piecemeal fashion, tackling problems one by one with no overall vision or direction guiding these attempts. Not surprisingly, this has led to solutions which appear to solve problems in one area only to create problems in another.

Baha'is recognise that human beings are social animals and need some basis for coming together in social groups. They need a common foundation and framework within which to interact with each other and a vision of what they are trying to achieve, the direction in which their society is headed. Before the 20th century, religion provided these. During the 20th century, various ideologies tried to provide these but failed. Today there is a vacuum at the centre of most societies. There is no agreed common basis or framework for social interactions, no vision of what the society is trying to achieve beyond some short-term political goals.

There seem to be two alternatives that are pressing for acceptance as the ideologies of the future. The first is religious fundamentalism and the second free market capitalism and western democracy.

Religious fundamentalism advocates that, following the failure of the modern man-made ideologies, the answer is to return to a time when traditional religion was the central ideology of society. Most of the failings of modern society – corruption, lack of sexual morality, crime, drugs, etc. – would, it is asserted, be solved if religious standards were more rigorously applied. This is not just a movement in the Islamic world but it has also shaped political thinking and attached itself to political parties in, for example, the United States and parts of Latin America, Israel, India and Sri Lanka.

However, it is not possible to turn the clock back and recreate the social situation of 200 years ago when religion was not just the ideology of a society, no other ideology was even conceivable. At that time, the religious construction of reality was the only reality for everyone. Once people have seen that there are alternative realities and that those alternative realities provide technological improvements that they rely on for their daily life, it is impossible to recreate the situation in which no alternative realities exist. In addition, religious fundamentalism fails to address the reason that religion was rejected in the first place: the fact that it was no longer seen to be relevant to the problems of the time nor in keeping with the modern world view. Further, evidence of the success of this approach is lacking. Societies that have adopted religious fundamentalism as their social and political framework are not noted for their adherence to human rights, their social advancement or even their effective handling of social issues such as drug abuse.

The second movement that some think can form the basis for the world's future is essentially an economic theory, free market capitalism coupled with western-style democracy. It is claimed that these can be a basis for social policy and provide a vision of where our societies should be heading. Many countries have adopted capitalism as their economic policy, even where democracy has not followed. However, capitalism it is not capable of forming an alternative social ideology since it is based on an individualistic philosophy that is the very antithesis of all concepts of society. The individualism that underlies free market capitalism dictates that social restrictions should be removed in order to allow the free operation of market forces. This philosophy relies on the greed and ambition of the individual as its motivating power. Some of its most ardent proponents have even asserted that there is no such thing as society and there are only individuals in competition with each other. Democracy has many more possibilities for providing a social framework. However, many political systems that call themselves democratic are clearly not and the influence of democracy has often been reduced merely to the holding of elections and the appearance of a multi-party system. Elections themselves are open to abuses and manipulation from vested interests and provide unedifying images of mud-slinging and misrepresentation for political advantage.

It is difficult, if not impossible, to build any form of social cohesion on the basis of such a philosophy. Indeed, those societies that have most enthusiastically adopted free market capitalism and western democracy have witnessed a loss of social cohesion and a resultant rise in social disaffection and alienation, as witnessed by increasing drug addiction, a rise in crime and anti-social behaviour, the development of a gun culture and gang warfare. Human beings are social animals and need a sense of belonging to a social group. If their society adopts an ideology that is destructive of this sense of social cohesion, then those who are at the fringes of the society demonstrate their disaffection and frustration by vandalism and crime and create their own social groupings such as gangs.

Thus there appear to be only two visions of the future of humanity: the one a materialistic and socially disruptive ideology that nevertheless retains some significant positive features, such as stressing the importance of human rights and freedoms, the importance of rational thought and science and the advancement of the position of women; the other is a religious ideology that seeks to return us to the past but also provides some significant positive values, such as the central importance of religion to society, the importance of the family and so on.

A third vision is what the Baha'i Faith offers. Part of what the Baha'i Faith is saying is that humanity needs to 're-vision' the basis for its social group. Throughout the 20th century, humans have pictured their nation as their social group. This is no longer an adequate basis for a world view. Humankind now needs to base itself on a vision of the 'world as one country' and itself as citizens of that country.

Baha'is believe that Baha'u'llah has given the framework for a socially cohesive, peaceful, prosperous, advanced and just society that can operate at all levels, locally, nationally and globally. Its distinctive characteristic is that it provides not only a vision of such a society but also the structures that enable such a society to be built and maintained over a long period.

The achievement of a future united world commonwealth will occur in two major stages, described by Baha'u'llah as the 'Lesser Peace' and the 'Most Great Peace'. The first is associated with a stage in human social development in which there will be a 'political unification of the Eastern and Western Hemispheres' and the 'emergence of a world government'. Baha'is believe this period has been prophesied not only by Baha'u'llah but also by the Prophet Isaiah (Shoghi Effendi, 1965, p. 33; Isa. 2:2–4; Isa. 9:6–7; Isa. 11:1–10); moreover, they believe that the foundations of the Lesser Peace were laid in the 20th century and that the world is presently in the process of implementing it. The Lesser Peace is not a period when the full fruits of Baha'u'llah's world order will be realised, but instead it will be a more limited 'political unity arrived at by decision of the governments of the various nations' (Universal House of Justice, 1985a). Its full realisation will, nevertheless, be a 'momentous and historic step' in the history of humankind and will require the 'reconstruction of mankind, as the result of the universal recognition of its oneness and wholeness' (Shoghi Effendi, 1980, p. 122).

Baha'u'llah offered the Lesser Peace to the world leaders of his day as a substitute for the Most Great Peace – 'a peace that must inevitably follow as the practical consequence of the spiritualization of the world and the fusion of all its races, creeds, classes and nations' (Shoghi Effendi, 1991, p. 162) – which they rejected: 'Now that ye have refused the Most Great Peace, hold ye fast unto this, the Lesser Peace, that haply ye may in some degree better your own condition and that of your dependents' (Bahá'u'lláh, 1983, p. 254). The period of the Most Great Peace will be so different from our present world that Baha'is hesitate even to describe it: 'To attempt to visualise it in all its possibilities, to estimate its future benefits, to picture its glory, would be premature at even so advanced a stage in the evolution of mankind. All we can reasonably venture to attempt is to strive to obtain a glimpse of the first streaks of the promised Dawn that must, in the fullness of time, chase away the gloom that has encircled humanity' (Shoghi Effendi, 1991, pp. 34–5).

Lesser Peace

Baha'is view the world as having evolved slowly and gradually through various stages of social unity, from the unification of the family, to the tribe, the city-state and the nation. Similarly, they consider that it is passing through various stages of social development, much as an individual passes through the different developmental stages of infancy, childhood, adolescence and eventually adulthood. They consider that humanity has already passed through its infancy and childhood, is coming to the end of its adolescence and will now attain its maturity. This period of the adulthood of the human race is equated with the universal recognition of the oneness of humanity, the establishment of the unity of the planet and the establishment of the Lesser Peace. It marks the last and highest stage in the evolution of humanity's collective life on the planet, the furthermost limits in the organisation of human society (ibid. p. 163). Just as humanity has gone through earlier phases of development, the Lesser Peace itself will develop in stages, with greater and greater degrees of unity and social justice being established in each stage. In the initial stages 'governments will act entirely on their own', but later the Baha'i Faith itself will begin to influence its processes (Universal House of Justice, 1985b). Just as adolescence is the most turbulent stage in the development of the individual, humanity as a whole has been experiencing a similar turbulence with wars, human crises of every description and a frustrating inability to deal effectively with change and modernisation. Not yet having the capacities, strategies or tools required to deal with such momentous, deeply rooted and widespread change, people resort to such knee-jerk responses as violence and terrorism, on the one hand, and increased government controls, on the other. Baha'is believe that the process of humanity's maturation requires a wholesale and organic change in every social institution and in the very structure of society itself (Shoghi Effendi, 1991, p. 43); moreover, it requires the creation of the machinery that can effectively manage a unified world. Failure to mature and to create such machinery jeopardises humanity's survival, just as the foolishness and impetuosity of the adolescent can put his future and even his life at risk if he does not become more wise, calm and mature.

In 1931 Shoghi Effendi described what would be required to move towards the Baha'i vision of a mature, smoothly functioning, united, prosperous, just and peaceful world community. He outlined the features and basic elements of the initial stages of its establishment, fully recognising the tremendous effort that will be required and without at all minimising or dismissing the obstacles that need to be overcome.

Underpinning the whole process is the recognition of the oneness and wholeness of humanity (Shoghi Effendi, 1980, p. 122). For many, this in itself presents a major obstacle that is impossible to overcome. Critics retort that people just do not see each other in this light, that there is an inherent antipathy between races and cultures and it will always be thus. The recognition of the oneness of humanity, Baha'is say, is already happening. The rapid evolution of transportation and communications over the last hundred years has revolutionised societies around the world, transforming them from often homogeneous communities to the multicultural, multi-ethnic, multi-religious cities and towns that are a feature of every country. Though in many cases still beset with problems, with different groups still maintaining a silo or ghetto mentality, as time moves on, as children continue to mix at school and people work together and marry across racial and ethnic lines, it becomes harder and harder to maintain the barriers that characterised an earlier stage of human development. Baha'is offer themselves, among others, as a model for how people of different races, religions, nationalities, languages, cultures, ethnicities, ages, genders and backgrounds can pay due respect to their own heritage and yet recognise their common humanity. The concept of 'unity in diversity' encapsulates, for Baha'is, the 'diversity of ethnical origins, of climate, of history, of language and tradition, of thought and habit, that differentiate the peoples and nations of the world' and which are neither to be ignored nor suppressed by subscribing to a wider loyalty to all humanity (Shoghi Effendi, 1991, p. 42).

Achievement of this vital and difficult stage will see the restructuring of many aspects of human life and the development of the international machinery necessary for the ordering and maintenance of a global community. Baha'is foresee the evolution of 'some form of a world super-state' (ibid. p. 40), led by a world government, a 'federal union' ('Abdu'l-Bahá, 1982, p. 167). Such an evolution is, however, not random but a measured and natural development of a human society that has moved from the social organisation of the family to the nation and is now moving on to a global society.

Critics baulk at the very notion of world government, citing the attempts of Hitler and Stalin to impose inhumane government on whole populations and the many fiction stories and novels that depict world government as a world tyranny with all its attendant anti-liberal restrictions. Yet Baha'is see such a world government as the inevitable and welcome outcome of processes already in train, a government that will foster a consciousness of unity and oneness which will provoke a sense of international collaboration and enable universal peace to be established whilst avoiding the dangers of political over-centralisation. It will have a federalist constitution and will comprise a number of democratic elements; moreover, it will be brought about by political will – that is, by the decision of the state governments – and will established through a treaty. It will not come about through military or economic action, force or coercion. Baha'is posit that such a government will not be imposed by one powerful country on all others, pointing out that all attempts to force such hegemony have proved impossible because they lack the consent of humanity, on the one hand, and the spiritual requirements of unity, on the other. Efforts by terrorists and Hitleresque figures to command world sovereignty are best prevented and defeated by willing governments acting together in a spirit of collective security.

In addition, the characteristics of the world government envisaged by Baha'is should be sufficient to counter the natural fears that such an unknown system engenders. Thus, for example, within this system, each state remains sovereign, although some elements of sovereignty are sacrificed to enable the world federal government to operate effectively, including the right of the state to act aggressively, unjustly and with impunity on the international stage wholly independently of other actors.

The value of such a world government is clear from a Baha'i perspective. A world government will secure political stability and peace for the world, thus enabling it to focus on eradicating poverty, fostering sustainable development and protecting the environment, overcoming natural disasters and promoting attitudes and behaviours at individual and collective levels that shun criminality and anti-social activities, such as drug abuse and human trafficking. Baha'is believe that the very tools that are used to invent the mechanisms that will bring peace can also be turned into sciences and arts that will benefit humanity. Once peace and unity are well established and a workable government is in place, the Baha'i writings suggest that the global economy will change to such an extent that the present gap created by wealth and poverty among nations and between people will be narrowed, and tax money presently used for defence and the war machine will be put to use for development, thereby increasing the prosperity of humanity in general.

Baha'is see the first step towards world government being the calling of a world summit to discuss world peace. Baha'is anticipate that the world leaders themselves will call and attend the summit and will conclude the necessary treaty creating the world government, although, from the Baha'i perspective, it is not necessary that all states agree to form the world government: only a 'certain number' need do so ('Abdu'l-Bahá, 1990, p. 64). It may be that such a summit will initially be called to reform the United Nations or to discuss some other global institutional development. However, the agenda items for the summit were identified by 'Abdu'l-Baha at the end of the 19th century: creating a 'union of the nations', reducing nationally held armaments, fixing national boundaries, determining how collective security will operate and setting out the principles of international law and how states will relate to one another (ibid. pp. 64–5). The treaty arising from the summit will, according to 'Abdu'l-Baha, be ratified 'by all the human race' (ibid. p. 64), perhaps through national referenda or some other electoral mechanism. Thus, Baha'is believe the world government will be established from the bottom up, not from the top down; will be created, not imposed; and will have its powers conferred by, not wrested from, national governments. In addition, the states that create the world government will be able to confer on it limited powers, although it is anticipated that the powers of the world government will increase as time moves on. However, in the nature of all federations, the principle of subsidiarity will apply; in other words, a higher authority should perform only those tasks that cannot be performed effectively at a lower level.

A significant step towards the creation of such a beneficial world government is, Shoghi Effendi says, 'the inevitable curtailment of unfettered national sovereignty' (Shoghi Effendi, 1991, p. 40). The key here is the willingness of states to do this: imposition of such a step will not result in the sort of world government envisaged by Baha'is. The willingness of states to take such a step will be strengthened, on the one hand, by self-interest – a clear-sighted realisation that the safety and survival of the state depend on this – and, on the other, by the fact that the government of that state is imbued with at least some of the ethical values, attitudes, behaviours and practices that Baha'u'llah describes as requirements of mature statesmanship.

The features of sovereignty which will need to be curtailed are:
- every claim to make war,
- 'certain rights to impose taxation', and
- 'all rights to maintain armaments, except for the purposes of maintaining internal order within their respective dominions'. (ibid. p. 40)

These are perhaps the most obvious rights for national governments to hand over to the control of a world government. The advantages of a war-free world are clear. Countries have been trying to limit the right of other nations to make war for many decades and have imposed various controls that restrict their abilities to go to war legally. That these have not wholly worked is, Baha'is point out, exactly why a more robust arrangement needs to be put in place. Both Baha'u'llah and his son 'Abdu'l-Baha deplored the heavy burden of tax imposed by intemperate and war-mongering rulers on their people, so it is not surprising to find these elements of national sovereignty curtailed. Restricting the stockpiling of weapons and decreasing the chances of war may have the added advantage of reducing taxes. At the same time, a world government will no doubt require funding and it is possible that taxes would need to be levied to provide this.

While this may seem an impossible achievement, the same elements of sovereignty were 'ceded', for example, by the individual states of the United States to its federal government. In return for this restriction of their sovereignty, the American states receive the protection of the federal government against invasion by other American states and foreign countries, and they are relieved of the need to hold huge stockpiles of armaments and to train large numbers of military personnel. They are freed from the requirement to mint their own money, nor do they need to negotiate with other countries over imports and exports of their products. Americans can move freely across state borders, can work anywhere in the United States that they can find a job, and can live in any state they like, taking advantage of that state's opportunities and facilities. Baha'is picture a similar situation in a federated world.

There are several democratic features of the anticipated world government worth mentioning. First, it will have a federalist constitution. Thus component states of the federation will *confer* rights and responsibilities on the world government, they will not be seized from them. Second, there will be a separation of powers into the judicial, legislative and executive branches of government. The federated world government would have three components:

- 'an international executive adequate to enforce supreme and unchallengeable authority on every recalcitrant member of the commonwealth;
- 'a world parliament whose members shall be elected by the people in their respective countries and whose election shall be confirmed by their respective governments;
- 'and a supreme tribunal whose judgement will have a binding effect even in such cases where the parties concerned did not voluntarily agree to submit their case to its consideration'. (ibid.)

The world executive 'corresponds to the executive head or board in present-day national governments' (Shoghi Effendi, 1934). The constitution will need to set out whether this is an elected or appointed body or individual. It is the elected legislature, rather than the executive, which is the locus of authority, as its members are considered 'the trustees of the whole of mankind' and it is intended that it will 'ultimately control the entire resources of all the component nations' (Shoghi Effendi, 1991, p. 203). The judiciary will be elected by the 'peoples and Governments of every nation' and will be 'composed of members elected from each country and Government' ('Abdu'l-Bahá, 1967, p. 155) and will thus be 'representative of all governments and peoples' ('Abdu'l-Bahá, 1978, p. 249). 'Abdu'l-Baha goes into some detail about how this election is to take place (ibid. p. 306).

The world government will be 'backed by an International force' (Shoghi Effendi, 1991, p. 203) – a police force or army – and will operate under a system of collective security:

> Be united, O kings of the earth, for thereby will the tempest of discord be stilled amongst you, and your people find rest, if ye be of them that comprehend. Should any one among you take up arms against another, rise ye all against him, for this is naught but manifest justice. *(Bahá'u'lláh, 1983, p. 254)*

Other democratic elements of the world government include: the autonomy of state members; universal suffrage; individual freedom; the freedom to act and 'to take individual initiative' ('Abdu'l-Bahá, 1978, p. 302; Shoghi Effendi, 1991, p. 203); freedom of the press 'from the influence of contending governments and peoples' (Shoghi Effendi, 1991, p. 204); equality of people before the law; the equality of women and men; protection of the rights of minorities; freedom of conscience (Shoghi Effendi, 1934; 'Abdu'l-Baha, 1980, p. 87); liberty of thought; the right of speech ('Abdu'l-Bahá, 1982, p. 197); and freedom of religion (Shoghi Effendi, 1980, p. 86).

Such a world government will require a high level of statesmanship and ethical conduct from its elected officials. Referring to the members of the world tribunal, 'Abdu'l-Baha indicated that only the 'choicest' ('Abdu'l-Bahá, 1978, p. 306) individuals are to serve, 'chosen from among the wisest and most judicious men of all the nations of the world' ('Abdu'l-Bahá, in *Star of the West*, 1914, p. 117). He identified the qualities necessary for those in government service as 'rectitude and honesty', 'temperance and self-discipline', 'purity and sanctity', 'justice and equity' ('Abdu'l-Bahá, in *Compilation*, 1991, vol. 2, p. 342). These qualities of leadership are identical to those virtues all individuals are to develop.

Baha'is hailed the creation of both the League of Nations and the United Nations as steps in the direction of world government but recognised their weaknesses and flaws. Today, Baha'is support the United Nations but consider that it is badly in need of reform and revitalisation and to this end have made a series of proposals (see Baha'i International Community, 1995b). Whether the UN can be recast as a federal government or reformed sufficiently to take on the tasks of world government, rather than remaining a meeting place of sovereign states – important as that is – is a possibility Baha'is do not dismiss. What is clear for Baha'is is that a world government must be capable of dealing effectively with the enormous changes that will occur as the world transforms itself into a united community and it must be strong enough to withstand the challenges to that process that will inevitably come from disaffected statesmen and individuals.

In 1936 Shoghi Effendi described the features of the world community he foresaw would gradually be established through the universal recognition of the oneness of humanity:

> A mechanism of world inter-communication will be devised, embracing the whole planet, freed from national hindrances and restrictions, and functioning with marvellous swiftness and perfect regularity. A world metropolis will act as the nerve centre of a world civilization, the focus towards which the unifying forces of life will converge and from which its energizing influences will radiate. A world language will either be invented or chosen from among the existing languages and will be taught in the schools of all the federated nations as an auxiliary to their mother tongue. A world script, a world literature, a uniform and universal system of currency, of weights and measures, will simplify and facilitate intercourse and understanding among the nations and races of mankind. *(Shoghi Effendi, 1991, p. 203)*

He also described the benefits and progress that will emerge as the world community advances and its functioning is perfected:

> In such a world society, science and religion, the two most potent forces in human life, will be reconciled, will cooperate, and will harmoniously develop. The press will, under such a system, while giving full scope to the expression of the diversified views and convictions of mankind, cease to be mischievously manipulated by vested interests, whether private or public, and will be liberated from the influence of contending governments and peoples. The economic resources of the

world will be organised, its sources of raw materials will be tapped and fully utilised, its markets will be coordinated and developed, and the distribution of its products will be equitably regulated.

National rivalries, hatreds, and intrigues will cease, and racial animosity and prejudice will be replaced by racial amity, understanding and cooperation. The causes of religious strife will be permanently removed, economic barriers and restrictions will be completely abolished, and the inordinate distinction between classes will be obliterated. Destitution on the one hand, and gross accumulation of ownership on the other, will disappear. The enormous energy dissipated and wasted on war, whether economic or political, will be consecrated to such ends as will extend the range of human inventions and technical development, to the increase of the productivity of mankind, to the extermination of disease, to the extension of scientific research, to the raising of the standard of physical health, to the sharpening and refinement of the human brain, to the exploitation of the unused and unsuspected resources of the planet, to the prolongation of human life, and to the furtherance of any other agency that can stimulate the intellectual, the moral, and spiritual life of the entire human race. *(ibid. pp. 203–4)*

Tools of the Lesser Peace

As humanity progresses towards and through the initial stages of the Lesser Peace, society will develop tools and create institutions and processes that will both help lay the groundwork for the Lesser Peace and stimulate further progress through it. Baha'u'llah identified a number of these, including the selection or creation of a universal auxiliary language and script, the determination of a universal standard for weights and measures, the creation of a single universal currency and the establishment of community 'storehouses' or financial repositories.

In his Kitab-i-Aqdas Baha'u'llah enjoins humanity to adopt a universal language and script, which 'will be the cause of unity' and the 'greatest instrument for promoting harmony and civilization' (Bahá'u'lláh, 1992, para. 189). There are two stages to this process: first, the selection or creation of a language by the world's governments to be taught to children around the world as an auxiliary language to their mother tongues; and second, much later, the adoption of a single language and script by everyone.

Similarly, the adoption of a single system of weights and measures will simplify manufacturing and other industrial processes and facilitate trade and international business. At a time when international financial markets are becoming ever more susceptible to fluctuation owing to world events, as national borders become more permeable and money moves more rapidly around the world, at the time when the European Union has established its own currency, and money laundering to support terrorism is rife, Baha'u'llah's call for a universal currency seems not only possible but practical and sensible. Not only would a universal currency end speculation in the money market, it would considerably ease business transactions and tend to narrow the gap between rich countries and poor.

'Abdu'l-Baha advanced the idea of establishing what he described as 'storehouses' in each village, town and city so that 'each individual member of the body politic will live most comfortably and happily under obligation to no one' ('Abdu'l-Bahá, 1945, p. 41). The idea of the storehouse, or financial repository, is that each person with an income contributes towards it, as a tithe. The storehouse also has other sources of revenue: income from animal husbandry and mining, the estates of those who die intestate and proceeds of any treasure trove found on the land. The storehouse is to be looked after by elected trustees and the beneficiaries are those who need emergency assistance, orphans, the disabled and incapacitated, the poor and elderly. Anything remaining in the storehouse after everyone is taken care of and all expenses are defrayed is to be sent to the national treasury. A more sophisticated and complex system will operate in large cities. This arrangement is one way to eliminate the present extremes of wealth and poverty that are so disruptive of social unity.

The Most Great Peace

The initial stages of the Lesser Peace are a 'political unity arrived at by the decision of the governments of various nations' (Universal House of Justice, 1985a). In this they act alone, without the conscious involvement of or direct action by the Baha'is, or through any plan or effort of the Baha'i community. Baha'is support the process – Baha'u'llah made it a duty of the Universal House of Justice to promote the Lesser Peace (Bahá'u'lláh, 1988b, p. 89) – but they are not directly involved in its evolution. The Baha'is see their role at this stage to be laying the groundwork for peace by promoting the principles of their religion and creating its institutions, thereby creating, on the one hand, the environment in which peace can be established and maintained and, on the other, developing agencies which will be the model for the future world society.

As the Lesser Peace takes shape and the world community becomes more firmly established, the Baha'i Faith and the teachings of Baha'u'llah will have a more direct role and influence on its development, offering counsel to the governments and sharing with them the model of Baha'i administration which, Baha'i believe, will form the pattern for the governance of the planet (Universal House of Justice, 1983).

Baha'is predict that the transformation of human society from its present condition through the Lesser Peace to the Most Great Peace will be long and gradual. While the world is going through this process, the Baha'i Faith itself will be passing through the different stages of its own development, both internally and externally: stages of 'unmitigated obscurity, of active repression, and of complete emancipation, leading in turn to its being acknowledged as an independent Faith, enjoying the status of full equality with its sister religions, to be followed by its establishment and recognition as a State religion, which in turn must give way to its assumption of the rights and prerogatives associated with the Baha'i state, functioning in the plenitude of its powers, a stage which must ultimately culminate in the emergence of the worldwide Baha'i Commonwealth, animated wholly by the spirit, and operating solely in direct conformity with the laws and principles of Baha'u'llah' (Shoghi Effendi, 1990, p. 15). The establishment of the Baha'i Commonwealth coincides with the 'Golden Age' of the Baha'i Faith, the attainment of the Most Great Peace and the 'flowering' of a world civilisation, 'divinely inspired, unique in its features, world-embracing in its scope, and fundamentally spiritual in its character' (Shoghi Effendi, 1971, p. 75).

The Spiritualised Society

The process of transformation from the present chaotic world society to the emergence of a fully functioning world commonwealth will be, Baha'is believe, complicated and lengthy and the road tortuous. During this long process there will be many pitfalls and challenges and it is expected that there will be reverses along the way. It is accepted that the early stages will not be conflict-free – hence the need for an international military or police force and limited armaments at the national level, along with the principle of collective security. Yet as society traverses this path, its members need to remain focused on their spiritual development as well as their social advancement.

Society itself needs to remain spiritualised throughout this long journey. Baha'u'llah himself warned that 'if carried to excess, civilization will prove as prolific a source of evil as it had been of goodness when kept within the restraints of moderation' (Bahá'u'lláh, 1983, p. 343). He reminded humanity that its purpose was to 'carry forward an ever-advancing civilization' and that the virtues individuals require as they do this are 'forbearance, mercy, compassion and loving-kindness towards all the peoples and kindreds of the earth' (ibid. p. 215), the same qualities needed at every stage in the individual's life. A spiritual society requires spiritual people who know themselves and know their Creator.

7

Baha'i Community Life

As described in Chapter 5, the teachings of Baha'u'llah seek to bring about a radical change in society: to change the present hierarchical societies to more egalitarian ones, based on a recognition of the oneness of humanity and driven by spiritual values. The structure and governance of the Baha'i community are designed to transform this vision into reality. While the communities of most religions have evolved gradually and almost accidentally over many centuries, responding to social forces, the Baha'i community has been deliberately created under the direct supervision of the founder of the Baha'i Faith and his successors so as to give physical form to the teachings of the religion.

The values, attitudes, behaviours and practices that underpin and drive the Baha'i community are the same as those that mould the Baha'i family at one end of the social spectrum and form the basis for the religion's vision of a workable global community at the other. Thus, in keeping with the Baha'i approach to the interconnectedness of all aspects of the religion and of life itself, the Baha'i community is not merely a structure designed to organise the affairs of the Baha'is but another location beyond the home where all the elements of the spiritual, physical, emotional, intellectual and educational needs of the individual, the family and Baha'i society are further nurtured and developed. It is also the place, other than the home, where the values, attitudes and behaviours promoted by the Baha'i Faith are most easily practised today. The same emphases appear in the community as appear in the home: values such as justice and unity, attitudes such as the importance of the devotional life, behaviours such as service to others, and practices such as consultation.

These themes give the Baha'i community some distinctive characteristics. Key among these are the equality of all members of the community, the governance of these communities, especially the system of elections and the decision-making process through consultation, and the Baha'i covenant, the 'glue' of the Baha'i Faith that creates and reinforces its unity.

Equality, Power and Authority

The starting principle of the organisation of the Baha'i community is that all individuals are equal. No individual is given a position where he or she has power or authority over others. With no religious professionals or community leaders in the Baha'i community, all authority resides in elected institutions. The community functions through consultation, which occurs both among the body of the Baha'is and also within the elected institutions. It is through consultation that all decisions are reached. Thus, the process of consultation is a primary activity and is central to an understanding of the operation of the Baha'i community.

The Baha'i Faith has no clergy, no religious professionals and no salaried theologians. Further, individuals do not hold power in the Baha'i community. Even those individuals who are elected onto the Baha'i institutions, or are appointed advisers, do not have any power or authority as individuals and are not distinguished by special clothing. Members of the national Baha'i governing council, the national spiritual assembly, for example, are under the authority of their local Baha'i institutions when participating in activities in their home communities. The individuals appointed within the administrative system are advisers to the elected institutions and are charged with assisting the propagation and protection of the religion.

While authority is vested in the elected institutions, power rests mainly with the body of believers in the Baha'i Faith. The institutions have only very limited powers to compel the Baha'is to follow their plans and instructions (their powers are usually only exercised in cases of individuals who have acted well outside the boundaries of what Baha'is consider acceptable behaviour). In general, the Baha'i institutions must win the support and cooperation of the generality of Baha'is in order to pursue their goals. Thus a very close and reciprocal relationship is built up between the Baha'i institutions and the generality of Baha'is, with Baha'is consulting together and offering suggestions and recommendations to their institutions and the institutions themselves consulting before arriving at their decisions. The Baha'is are motivated to carry out these plans because of their love for their religion, the unity that has been created among them, their desire to see their religion progress, their faithfulness to the 'covenant' of Baha'u'llah and because they have been involved in the process of drawing up the plans themselves.

Furthermore, as indicated in Chapter 1, the Baha'i community is a mystic community and its structures of governance reflect this. Thus, the very functioning of the Baha'i community is designed to assist the

spiritual development of the individual. The same process of consultation that helps to promote a more egalitarian society, where everyone
feels that they have a say and are involved in decision-making, also
promotes the spiritual development of the individual. Thus the
administrative, the social and the spiritual are all interconnected and
interdependent.

The Covenant

Unity is the hallmark of the teachings of Baha'u'llah. He calls for the
unity of humanity, for recognition of the unity of God and of his manifestations, for the unity of sexes and for unity of action after a decision
has been made in consultation. It is the covenant that provides the
unity of the Baha'i Faith itself.

The basic meaning of the word 'covenant' is that of a contract or
binding agreement. The scriptures of the world have referred to the
spiritual contract binding God and humanity. The Baha'i Faith
recognises two covenants: first, the greater covenant between God,
represented by the Manifestation of God, on the one hand, and
humanity on the other, in which God promises to continue to send
guidance to humankind, while humanity, on its part, promises to obey
and follow these teachings when they come. Part of this greater
covenant is the obligation which each Manifestation of God places
upon his followers to accept the next Manifestation. This takes the
form, for example, of Christ's promise that he will return, and of the
promise made by Baha'u'llah that there will be another Manifestation
of God in a thousand years.

However, in the Baha'i teachings, there is a second, lesser
covenant, which obliges individual Baha'is to accept the leadership of
Baha'u'llah's appointed successors and the administrative institutions
of the Faith. Because of the paramount importance of the teaching of
the unity of humankind in the Baha'i Faith, it is clearly necessary that
the Baha'i community itself should remain united. This covenant therefore concerns the question of leadership and authority in the Baha'i
community and it is the pivot and guarantor of unity in the Baha'i
community. Its central purpose is to prevent schism and dissension.

Although precedents for this type of covenant may exist in other
religions, Shoghi Effendi asserts that in no previous religion has the
question of the succession been of such importance nor the
appointment of the successor been so clearly made. The fact that the
succession to the authority and central institutions of the Baha'i Faith
were established by written documents so that they could not later be

> Inasmuch as great differences and divergences of denomina-
> tional belief had arisen throughout the past, every man with a
> new idea attributing it to God, Bahá'u'lláh desired that there
> should not be any ground or reason for disagreement among
> the Bahá'ís. Therefore, with His own pen He wrote the Book of
> His Covenant, addressing His relations and all people of the
> world, saying, 'Verily, I have appointed One Who is the Center
> of My Covenant. All must obey Him; all must turn to Him; He is
> the Expounder of My Book, and He is informed of My purpose.
> All must turn to Him. Whatsoever He says is correct, for, verily,
> He knoweth the texts of My Book. Other than He, no one doth
> know My Book.' The purpose of this statement is that there
> should never be discord and divergence among the Baha'is but
> that they should always be unified and agreed. ('Abdu'l-Bahá,
> 1982, pp. 322–3)

questioned is emphasised by Shoghi Effendi as a 'distinguishing
feature' of the religion of Baha'u'llah (Shoghi Effendi, 1991, pp.
21–2).

The central authority in the Baha'i Faith was delegated by
Baha'u'llah in his written will and testament to his son 'Abdu'l-Baha,
who was thus called the Centre of the Covenant. 'Abdu'l-Baha was
also appointed the authorised interpreter of the writings of Baha-
'u'llah. 'Abdu'l-Baha then conferred this central authority and the
position of authorised interpreter of the Baha'i scriptures upon Shoghi
Effendi in his written will and testament, instructing the latter to
establish the Universal House of Justice, a body that had been
described in the writings of Baha'u'llah. It took Shoghi Effendi the
whole of his ministry to set up the local and national Baha'i adminis-
trations and to get them functioning in such a manner as would permit
the election of the Universal House of Justice. Shoghi Effendi passed
away in 1957 and in 1963 the first Universal House of Justice was
elected, which has from that time on been the central authority in the
Baha'i community. Baha'u'llah also gave the Universal House of
Justice the authority to legislate on those matters on which there were
no specific instructions in the Baha'i scriptures.

> The provenance, the authority, the duties, the sphere of
> action of the Universal House of Justice all derive from the
> revealed Word of Bahá'u'lláh, which, together with the inter-
> pretations and expositions of the Centre of the Covenant and
> of the Guardian of the Cause – who, after 'Abdu'l-Bahá, is
> the sole authority in the interpretation of Bahá'í Scripture –
> constitute the binding terms of reference of the Universal

House of Justice and are its bedrock foundation. The authority of these Texts is absolute and immutable until such time as
Almighty God shall reveal His new Manifestation to Whom
will belong all authority and power. *(Universal House of Justice,
1972, pp. 3–4)*

Firmness in this covenant is therefore one of the chief Baha'i religious
virtues and includes not just acceptance of the legitimacy of the Baha'i
institutions but much more general attitudes of loyalty and whole-
hearted commitment to the Baha'i Faith and the Baha'i community.
Challenging the authority of the centre of the Baha'i Faith is the most
serious spiritual offence that a Baha'i can commit. It is considered to be
a spiritual disease and is punished by expulsion from the community.

In its more general sense, firmness in the covenant means carrying
out the laws and teachings of the Baha'i Faith.

> . . . ye must conduct yourselves in such a manner that ye may
> stand out distinguished and brilliant as the sun among other
> souls. Should any one of you enter a city, he should become a
> center of attraction by reason of his sincerity, his faithfulness
> and love, his honesty and fidelity, his truthfulness and
> loving-kindness towards all the peoples of the world . . . Not
> until ye attain this station can ye be said to have been faithful
> to the Covenant and Testament of God. For He hath,
> through irrefutable Texts, entered into a binding Covenant
> with us all, requiring us to act in accordance with His sacred
> instructions and counsels. *('Abdu'l-Bahá, 1978, p. 71)*

In a more specific sense, firmness in the covenant refers to the
inner conviction of the individual Baha'i that the guidance of the
centre of the Baha'i Faith (whether 'Abdu'l-Baha or Shoghi Effendi in
the past, or the Universal House of Justice at present) represents the
will of God: 'Whatsoever they decide is of God' ('Abdu'l-Bahá, 1991,
p. 11). Shoghi Effendi relates the success and progress of the Baha'i
Faith to this:

> Neither the administration, nor the general teaching work of
> the Cause . . . will progress, or be able to accomplish
> anything, unless the believers are truly firm, deep, spiritually
> convinced Baha'is . . . once a Baha'i has the profound convic-
> tion of the *authority* from God, vested in the Prophet, passed
> on to the Master, and by Him, to the Guardians, and which
> flows out through the assemblies and creates order based on
> obedience – once a Baha'i has this, nothing can shake him.
> *(Shoghi Effendi, 1949)*

The importance of the doctrine of the covenant can be seen in the fact that the very identity of a Baha'i is linked to it: to be a Baha'i means to turn to the Universal House of Justice as the ultimate source of authority in the Baha'i Faith.

Some have claimed that this doctrine of the covenant leads to an authoritarian structure in the Baha'i Faith (the word totalitarian has even been used), which is the very opposite of the egalitarian society free of hierarchical structures that is the aim of the Baha'i Faith. There are two aspects to consider in order to understand why this is not a correct assessment. Both of these are bound up with the fact that in the Baha'i community, unlike almost every other human institution, there is a separation between authority and power.

The first aspect relates to the fact that, although the elected institutions of the Baha'i community have the authority to direct the affairs of the community – and in theory the doctrine of the covenant gives to them, and especially to the Universal House of Justice, great authority – the obligation of these institutions is to try to achieve their objectives through winning the support of individual Baha'is. Although primarily addressing the members of the elected Baha'i institutions, Shoghi Effendi states:

> Let us also bear in mind that the keynote of the Cause of God is not dictatorial authority but humble fellowship, not arbitrary power, but the spirit of frank and loving consultation. Nothing short of the spirit of a true Baha'i can hope to reconcile the principles of mercy and justice, of freedom and submission, of the sanctity of the right of the individual and of self-surrender, of vigilance, discretion and prudence on the one hand, and fellowship, candor, and courage on the other. *(Shoghi Effendi, 1968, pp. 63–4)*

The elected Baha'i institutions have in effect very little power to enforce their authority in many areas when compared with the central authorities of other religions. They have no doctrinal authority; no authority to determine correct doctrine or to create new doctrine or theological teachings nor to interpret the texts of the scripture. Thus they hold no power in many areas over which religious leadership has traditionally held both power and authority. They have the authority to direct the Baha'i community by laying out plans of action for Baha'is, but they have no sanctions or other means of compelling Baha'is to carry out these plans. If any Baha'i, for example, wants to ignore completely the present Five Year Plan of the Universal House of Justice, he is free to do so without any fear of sanctions against him. The general situation is summed up in the words of the Universal

House of Justice thus: 'Authority and direction flow from the Assemblies, whereas the power to accomplish the tasks resides primarily in the entire body of the believers' (Universal House of Justice, 1969).

The second aspect arises from the fact that, paradoxically, the doctrine of the covenant, while appearing to give great authority to the institutions of the Baha'i Faith, at the same time gives great freedom to the individual Baha'i. Provided that individual Baha'is abide by the provisions of the covenant, they have a great amount of freedom in other areas. They are free to read the scriptures and interpret these for themselves (as long as they do not try to set up sectarian divisions by claiming authority for their interpretations). They are free to decide the extent to which they involve themselves in the Baha'i community. They are free to decide what financial contributions they make to the Baha'i funds. They are free to decide to what extent they obey the Baha'i laws regarding such matters as prayer and fasting. They are free to decide to what extent they follow the moral and ethical guidelines given in the Baha'i scriptures (although flagrant immorality which brings the community into disrepute may be sanctioned).

Governance: Baha'i Administration

Baha'is call their system of governance the 'administrative order' or simply the 'Baha'i administration'. Baha'u'llah himself established the outlines of the administrative order in the Kitab-i-Aqdas and in his other writings and these were fleshed out and brought into being by 'Abdu'l-Baha and Shoghi Effendi. The administrative order is an integral part of the Baha'i religion and cannot be separated from it:

> Regarding the relationship of the Cause to the Administration; the Baha'i Faith as the Guardian himself has repeatedly and emphatically stated cannot be confined to a mere system of organization, however elaborate in its features and universal in its scope it may be. Organization is only a means to the realization of its aims and ideals, and not an end in itself. To divorce the two, however, would be to mutilate the Cause itself, as they stand inseparably bound to each other, in very much the same relationship existing between the soul and body in the world of human existence. *(Shoghi Effendi, 1939a)*

The purpose of the administrative order 'is primarily to lend strength and directive to the teaching work and to promote the establishment of the Faith. It should never be regarded as an end in itself but purely as a means to canalise and make effective a spiritual vitality generated by the Word of God in the hearts of the believers' (Universal House of Justice, 1973). Baha'is believe that the institutions they are creating, and which are even now only embryonic in form, will eventually evolve into the governance system of the wider community:

> This Cause is a Cause which God has revealed to humanity as a whole. It is designed to benefit the entire human race, and the only way it can do this is to re-form the community life of mankind, as well as seeking to regenerate the individual. The Baha'i Administration is only the first shaping of what in future will come to be the social life and laws of community living. *(Shoghi Effendi, 1941)*

Baha'i administration runs in two parallel channels which complement each other. On the one hand are the elected institutions, termed by Baha'u'llah the 'rulers': the Universal House of Justice, national spiritual assemblies and local spiritual assemblies. Recently, the Universal House of Justice has called for the election of regional Baha'i councils in some countries, situated between local and national assemblies. On the other hand are the appointed institutions, termed by Baha'u'llah the 'learned': the Guardian of the Faith, the Hands of the Cause of God, the Counsellors of the International Teaching Centre, the Continental Boards of Counsellors, the Auxiliary Board members and their assistants. These individuals are charged with assisting the propagation and protection of the religion and are advisers to the elected institutions and, where appropriate, to individual Baha'is.

The Universal House of Justice

Baha'u'llah provided for the establishment of the Universal House of Justice in the Kitab-i-Aqdas. The supreme administrative body of the Baha'i Faith was elected for the first time in 1963. The Universal House of Justice is the head of the Baha'i Faith and on it rests the ultimate responsibility for ensuring its unity and progress.

The Universal House of Justice has a number of powers and duties, a summary of which can be found in its constitution. Among these are 'to enact laws and ordinances not expressly recorded in the Sacred Texts; to abrogate, according to the changes and requirements of the time, its own enactments; to deliberate and decide upon all problems which have caused difference; to elucidate questions that are obscure; to safeguard the personal rights, freedom and initiative of individuals' (Universal House of Justice, 1972).

The men of God's House of Justice have been charged with the affairs of the people. They, in truth, are the Trustees of God among His servants and the daysprings of authority in His countries . . . Inasmuch as for each day there is a new problem and for every problem an expedient solution, such affairs should be referred to the Ministers of the House of Justice that they may act according to the needs and requirements of the time . . . It is incumbent upon all to be obedient unto them. *(Bahá'u'lláh, 1988b, pp. 26–7)*

Baha'is believe the decisions of the Universal House of Justice to be infallible. In his Will and Testament 'Abdu'l-Baha stated that both the Guardian and the Universal House of Justice are 'under the care and protection of the Abhá Beauty [Baha'u'llah], under the shelter and unerring guidance of the Exalted One . . . [the Bab]' ('Abdu'l- Bahá, 1991, p. 11). 'Abdu'l-Baha explained the nature of this infallibility:

. . . essential infallibility belongs especially to the supreme Manifestations, and acquired infallibility is granted to every holy soul. For instance, the Universal House of Justice, if it be established under the necessary conditions – with members elected from all the people – that House of Justice will be under the protection and the unerring guidance of God. If that House of Justice shall decide unanimously, or by a majority, upon any question not mentioned in the Book, that decision and command will be guarded from mistake. Now the members of the House of Justice have not, individually, essential infallibility; but the body of the House of Justice is under the protection and unerring guidance of God: this is called conferred infallibility. *('Abdu'l-Bahá, 1981, pp. 172–3)*

Membership of the Universal House of Justice is confined to men and is at present fixed at nine. The House of Justice is elected every five years at an international convention held during the Ridvan period.

National Spiritual Assemblies

In his Will and Testament 'Abdu'l-Baha established 'secondary Houses of Justice', today called national spiritual assemblies, or, where they administer a wider area, regional spiritual assemblies. The first national spiritual assemblies, in the British Isles, Germany and Austria, and India and Burma, were elected in 1923. There are at the time of writing over 180 national spiritual assemblies.

The national spiritual assembly oversees the administration, teaching work and activities of a national Baha'i community. Its decisions are not infallible. Its nine members are elected annually at a national convention held during the Ridvan period and serve for one year, although individuals may be elected to serve many times.

Local Spiritual Assemblies

In every town or city where there are nine or more adult Baha'is, Baha'u'llah called for the formation of local houses of justice:

> The Lord hath ordained that in every city a House of Justice be established wherein shall gather counsellors to the number of Bahá [nine], and should it exceed this number it doth not matter. They should consider themselves as entering the Court of the presence of God, the Exalted, the Most High, and as beholding Him Who is the Unseen. It behoveth them to be the trusted ones of the Merciful among men and to regard themselves as the guardians appointed of God for all that dwell on earth. It is incumbent upon them to take counsel together and to have regard for the interests of the servants of God, for His sake, even as they regard their own interests, and to choose that which is meet and seemly. Thus hath the Lord your God commanded you. *(Bahá'u'lláh, 1992, para. 30)*

These elected institutions are at present called local spiritual assemblies, reflecting their embryonic nature and limited powers at this point in their evolution. The first local spiritual assemblies were established at the end of the 19th century. At the time of writing there are more than 10,300 around the world.

The nine members of the assembly are directly elected from among all the adult believers in the local community every Ridvan and serve for one year, although they may be elected year after year. The assembly oversees the teaching and other work of the Baha'i community, arranges the 19-day feast and commemorations of holy days, conducts marriages and funerals, provides for the Baha'i education of children and offers advice, guidance and assistance for those in difficulty. All its decisions are taken after consultation but its decisions are not infallible. Individual Baha'is have the right to appeal decisions of their local assembly to the national assembly and even the decisions of their national assembly to the Universal House of Justice. But once the Universal House of Justice has decided a matter, then the doctrine of the covenant requires all Baha'is to submit to this decision.

Regional Baha'i Councils

In those countries where there are large numbers of Baha'is and local assemblies or where the administration of the national Baha'i community is complex and the Baha'i institutions mature, the Universal House of Justice has called for the election of regional Baha'i councils to take on some responsibilities for the administration and propagation of the religion. They function between local spiritual assemblies and the national spiritual assembly and provide for a level of autonomous decision-making on a range of issues devolved to them by the national assembly. The role of the regional Baha'i councils continues to evolve and increasing numbers of national communities are establishing them.

The Guardianship

'Abdu'l-Baha established the Guardianship in his Will and Testament and appointed Shoghi Effendi as the first Guardian. The Guardian was to act as sole interpreter of the Baha'i scriptures and to be the permanent head for life of the Universal House of Justice. His successor was to be his first-born son or another male member of the family of Baha'u'llah. However, Shoghi Effendi died in 1957 without children and there were no male members to appoint, thus there are no more Guardians.

As head of the Baha'i Faith, Shoghi Effendi was responsible for the religion's development and propagation. As the Universal House of Justice was not established during his lifetime, a primary area of work was to increase the number of Baha'is worldwide and to assist them to elect the local and national assemblies that formed the foundation for the election of the House of Justice. He launched major international campaigns that took the religion to all parts of the world and at the same time preserved the unity of the Baha'i Faith and protected it against attacks and persecution.

Shoghi Effendi undertook the major task of translating into English many of the writings and prayers of Baha'u'llah, including 184 prayers and meditations collected into one volume and a compilation of 165 passages from other writings of Baha'u'llah in the volume *Gleanings from the Writings of Bahá'u'lláh*. He also translated Nabil-i-A'zam's history of the Babi movement, *The Dawn-Breakers*, and passages from the talks of 'Abdu'l-Baha. Although he wrote only one book, *God Passes By*, a history of the first hundred years of the Baha'i Faith, compilations of his letters of guidance are published as books and some of the letters themselves, such as *The Advent of Divine Justice*, are of book length.

At the same time Shoghi Effendi developed the Baha'i shrines and properties in the Holy Land, erecting the shrine of the Bab on Mount Carmel and personally laying out and beautifying the gardens around it.

After Shoghi Effendi's death the Hands of the Cause took on the responsibility for guiding and leading the Baha'i community until the Universal House of Justice could be elected.

Hands of the Cause

Baha'u'llah appointed Hands of the Cause, distinguished Baha'is who were charged with the protection and propagation of the religion. 'Abdu'l-Baha also appointed Hands of the Cause and further developed the institution in his Will and Testament, providing that the Guardian should nominate and appoint future Hands. Shoghi Effendi appointed a number of Hands but after his passing no further Hands could be appointed. At present, there is only one living Hand of the Cause.

International Teaching Centre

The Universal House of Justice established the International Teaching Centre in 1973 to bring to fruition the work of the Hands of the Cause and to provide for its extension into the future. The Teaching Centre coordinates, guides and directs the work of the Continental Boards of Counsellors and makes recommendations to the Universal House of Justice regarding the direction of the teaching work worldwide. The members of the International Teaching Centre are appointed by the Universal House of Justice. The Counsellors who make up the International Teaching Centre are appointed for five-year terms.

Continental Boards of Counsellors

In 1968 the Universal House of Justice created the Continental Boards of Counsellors to extend into the future the work of the Hands of the Cause to protect and propagate the Baha'i Faith. The duties of the Counsellors include directing the work of the Auxiliary Boards, consulting and collaborating with national spiritual assemblies and keeping the Universal House of Justice and the International Teaching Centre informed of the condition of the religion in their countries. Counsellors are appointed for terms of five years and function as Counsellors only when in the continent to which they have been appointed.

Auxiliary Boards and their Assistants

Shoghi Effendi created the Auxiliary Boards in 1954 to assist the Hands of the Cause. In 1968 the Universal House of Justice placed them under the direction of the Continental Boards of Counsellors, who appoint them from among the Baha'is living in their geographical zone. Each zone has two boards. The protection boards protect the Faith from attacks, encourage the believers to deepen their knowledge of the Faith and promote unity. The propagation boards promote teaching work and the training institute process. Auxiliary Boards may appoint assistants to work with local communities or sections of the community, such as youth. Auxiliary Board members and their assistants do not make administrative decisions or judgements but offer advice and counsel.

Baha'i Elections

While most elections in the world today are highly competitive and are too often manipulated so as to maintain certain groups in power, Baha'i elections are run by very different processes that do not reinforce the hierarchical nature of society and that respect the spiritual values on which the religion is founded. Baha'is consider their elections to be part of a divine process, one that will ultimately aid in establishing justice in the world. Participating in Baha'i elections is seen as a sacred responsibility and even those who are not themselves voting are encouraged to participate in and contribute to the process by praying for the guidance of the electors.

Baha'i elections are held in a manner that does not encourage divisiveness or competitiveness. They are conducted by secret ballot, without nominations, canvassing or any form of electioneering. No one 'stands' for election and thus there are no candidates, political parties, election pledges, rallies, manifestos, platforms or campaigns. Indeed, there is no discussion at all of personalities before an election or of a person's views, policies, beliefs or stance on any particular subject. The only discussion permissible is about 'the qualities and requirements of office' (Shoghi Effendi, 1933a): 'Hence it is incumbent upon the chosen delegates to consider without the least trace of passion and prejudice, and irrespective of any material consideration, the names of only those who can best combine the necessary qualities of unquestioned loyalty, of selfless devotion, of a well-trained mind, of recognised ability and mature experience' (Shoghi Effendi, 1968, p. 88). It is not permitted to discuss even whether any particular person has such qualities.

However, the purpose of Baha'i elections is not only to elect those who will administer the Baha'i community in the coming year but also to develop in individual electors the 'spirit of responsibility' (Shoghi Effendi, 1935a). Thus Baha'is are to be well-informed, active members of their community and to get to know everyone in it well enough to be able to consider for themselves whether they have the appropriate qualities for membership of the institution being elected. This is clearly challenging for those voting in elections at the national and international levels, but it remains the duty of every Baha'i 'to become an intelligent, well-informed and responsible elector' (ibid.).

The election itself is generally held at a special meeting called for the purpose. Elections for the Universal House of Justice, national spiritual assemblies and local spiritual assemblies are held during the Festival of Ridvan. Except where circumstances make it impossible, local spiritual assemblies are elected on the first day of Ridvan, from sunset on 20 April until sunset on 21 April. National spiritual assemblies are elected at some time during the 12 days of Ridvan at a national convention. The Universal House of Justice is, at present, elected every five years during the Ridvan period at an international convention convened in Haifa. In 2003 circumstances in the Middle East made it too dangerous to convene the international convention and the election of the Universal House of Justice was held by postal ballot. Regional Baha'i councils are at present elected in the autumn, either at specially convened meetings or by postal ballot.

The spirit of the electors is as important as their freedom to choose among all the eligible Baha'is living in the relevant jurisdiction. Elections are held in a reverent atmosphere, the electors 'prayerfully and devotedly and after meditation and reflection' voting only for those 'faithful, sincere, experienced, capable and competent souls who are worthy of membership' (Shoghi Effendi, 1943).

To vote, the elector simply writes down the names of those individuals (at present, nine for local and national spiritual assemblies, regional Baha'i councils and the Universal House of Justice, generally one for the election of delegates to the national convention) whom he feels are most suitable for service. Those people with the highest number of votes assume office.

Notwithstanding the freedom of electors to vote for anyone eligible, regardless of background, gender or ethnicity, an interesting feature of Baha'i elections is the principle of positive discrimination that applies when there are tied votes for ninth place: if one person is from a minority group, 'priority should unhesitatingly be accorded the party representing the minority' (Shoghi Effendi, 1990, p. 35).

Every adult Baha'i has the right to participate in the processes that establish the Faith's elected institutions. All adult Baha'is in good standing in a specific locality are eligible to vote for, and to be elected to, the local spiritual assembly. All adult Baha'is living in the area covered by a regional Baha'i council are eligible to be elected to the regional council; regional Baha'i councils are elected by members of the local spiritual assemblies established in the area of its jurisdiction. All adult Baha'is living in a particular electoral unit are eligible to vote for, and to be elected as, a delegate to the national convention. Delegates to the national convention vote for members of the national spiritual assembly. Every adult Baha'i in a country is eligible for election to the national assembly, not just delegates. National spiritual assembly members elect the members of the Universal House of Justice from among the adult male Baha'is of the world community. This last consideration has proved a puzzling feature for many who look at the teachings of the Baha'i Faith on the equality of women and men. For the present, Baha'is have to take it on faith that the wisdom of this measure will in the future become 'manifest as the sun at high noon' ('Abdu'l-Bahá, 1978, p. 80).

Local and national assemblies and regional councils elect their officers from among their own number. The election of officers is conducted in the same way as other Baha'i elections except that a person must receive at least five votes to assume office. The Universal House of Justice has no permanent officers.

'Abdu'l-Baha emphasised that elected Baha'i assemblies are 'under the guidance and protection of God' but that the people who compose them are human beings 'subject to the same human limitations that characterise the other members of the community'. It is for this reason that they have to be elected every year – so that the community has an 'opportunity to remedy any defect or imperfection' and 'the quality of membership in Baha'i Assemblies can be continually raised and improved' (Shoghi Effendi, 1935c).

Consultation

Consultation is the process of decision-making, discussion and sharing ideas advocated by Baha'u'llah. All decisions, large and small, made by Baha'is within their homes, communities and administrative institutions are to be made through the process of consultation. As generally practised in society, consultation has become discredited as a way of making decisions by appearing to take into account the views of others while in reality pushing through predetermined agendas. This is not what is meant by the word 'consultation' in the Baha'i Faith and so this process is considered in depth in this chapter.

> **Take ye counsel together in all matters, inasmuch as consultation is the lamp of guidance which leadeth the way, and is the bestower of understanding.** (Bahá'u'lláh, 1988b, p. 168)

For Baha'is, consultation is a spiritual process that is much more than merely the making of decisions, however important. At one level, it is a dynamic, purposeful way to discuss issues and share ideas. At another, it is intended to help people solve problems and deal with personal difficulties. At yet another, it is a way for individuals, families and communities to plan courses of action and find the resources for carrying them out. Beyond this, consultation is a way of creating unity and at the same time providing a place where all the values, attitudes and behaviours prized by Baha'is can be practised and are most evident. Further, consultative processes are designed to ensure that every member of the community – women, members of minority groups, the poor and all of those who do not get heard in our present society – have an input into the process.

Consultation from the Baha'i perspective is a key way of reinforcing the non-hierarchical social framework postulated by Baha'u'llah. It reflects the social principles of the religion that call for justice, participation, the equality of all people, social responsibility and the search for truth, coupled with spiritual values such as trustworthiness, love, patience, courtesy and mindfulness. Consultation, Baha'is maintain, lies at the very foundation of a properly run society and is at the heart of good governance.

Those engaged in consultation are to bring a number spiritual qualities to the process, as well as a range of skills. The very process of consultation can evoke these qualities and assist in their refinement. 'Abdu'l-Baha stated that the 'prime requisites' for those who consult are 'purity of motive, radiance of spirit, detachment from all else save God, attraction to His Divine Fragrances, humility and lowliness amongst His loved ones, patience and long-suffering in difficulties and servitude to His exalted Threshold' ('Abdu'l-Bahá, 1978, p. 87). This involves listening carefully and mindfully to all points of view; offering one's own contribution with candour, courtesy and dignity; having a calm approach; being open-minded; upholding freedom of thought; and wholeheartedly accepting a majority decision. The atmosphere in which all this takes place is, ideally, one of love and harmony with all participants turning towards God in prayer and asking His assistance. 'Abdu'l-Baha states that those consulting 'must then proceed with the utmost devotion, courtesy, dignity, care and moderation to express their views. They must in every matter search out the truth and not insist upon their own opinion, for stubbornness and persistence in one's views will lead ultimately to discord and wrangling and the truth will remain hidden . . . it is in no wise permissible for one to belittle the thought of another . . .' (ibid. p. 88).

The Baha'i writings describe the steps in the process of consultation: ascertaining the facts of the situation, deciding what spiritual principles apply, researching the Baha'i writings for insights and guidance, having a thoughtful and open-minded discussion, coming to a conclusion, making a decision – by taking a vote, if necessary – and implementing the decision. In practice, gathering and ascertaining the facts is often the most difficult step, as deciding what is relevant and what is not is an important part of the process.

The spiritual atmosphere of consultation is maintained in the way suggestions are to be made and ideas put forward. A distinctive feature of the discussion is that the person making a suggestion immediately detaches himself from it – that is, it becomes one of a number of ideas put forward and is to be consulted upon dispassionately and objectively, even by the person who advocates it. If the consulting group does not take up the idea, the proposer does not continue to promote it but moves on, listening carefully to other points of view. It is intended that every idea be offered, and received, with humility and in a spirit of contributing to the whole. It is the very nature of the consultation process that an idea will be modified and built upon by subsequent speakers. It is taken as read that no one coming into the consultation process expects his or her own ideas to prevail and it is against the spirit of consultation for a participant to try to influence others unduly, to use threats or emotional blackmail, or to 'hang onto' his or her own ideas.

As the discussion continues, the issues become clear and the spiritual principles involved are identified, often a conclusion about the situation emerges. A participant may at this point offer a tentative resolution. If this meets with universal approval, a decision is made and discussion on that point ends. If not, the discussion continues using the above principles until consensus is reached or, if there is still disagreement, a vote is taken.

Voting is a last resort, as consensus is valued. Should a vote be required, every participant has a single vote; the chairman does not have a casting vote, again emphasising the non-hierarchical nature of Baha'i society. Only votes in favour of a proposition are counted: there is no vote 'against' a proposition and there are no abstentions – a person who does not vote for a proposition is considered to have, in effect, voted against it. A simple majority is sufficient to make the decision. There are no vetoes.

A decision taken, even by a majority vote, is considered to be the decision of everyone and all are expected to uphold it, including those who may not have supported it up to this point. There are no minority opinions and no one must criticise the decision, either in or out of the meeting. Baha'is view such criticism as undermining the implementation of the decision. 'Abdu'l-Baha indicated that, as unity is the highest aspiration of Baha'is, a decision taken and implemented in unity, even if wrong, is preferable to one that is created and implemented in disunity. A wrong decision taken and implemented in unity can readily be seen to be flawed and immediately corrected, whereas when a decision is criticised and not upheld by everyone, it is impossible to determine whether the decision itself was incorrect or whether it did not produce a satisfactory outcome because it was not supported by everyone.

The implementation of the decision is part of the consultation process. A decision, no matter how thoroughly discussed and no matter how united the decision, is of no use if it is not acted upon.

Ideally, Baha'i consultation provides a safe and encouraging environment for people to express their views. In the cooperative environment produced by the consultation process, people often marginalised in the wider society feel comfortable and valued putting forward their opinions. Thus, for example, women, who in many societies do not take an active part in governance or any decision-making forums, are able to play a major role in Baha'i community life.

Consultation is used in a variety of settings among Baha'is and for many situations. All Baha'i institutions use consultation to make every decision. Members of local Baha'i communities come together every month at the 19-day feast, a third of which is devoted to consultation. Marriage partners use consultation to make decisions and formulate plans, although as there are only two participants involved, clearly a vote is not possible and, should the parties continue to disagree, sometimes the views of one and sometimes those of the other should prevail. Baha'i families are encouraged to use consultation as appropriate and to teach the spiritual qualities, attitudes and skills required to their children. Individuals are to consult with family, friends or Baha'i institutions before making important decisions, and 'the members of each profession, such as in industry, should consult, and those in commerce should similarly consult on business affairs' ('Abdu'l-Bahá, cited in Shoghi Effendi, 1922). Even those in leadership roles within the community, who have the authority and responsibility to make autonomous decisions, such as company directors or school principals, often consult with others before making a final decision and acting.

Community Life

Individual Baha'is and Baha'i families are part of a network of Baha'i communities around the world, organised at the local, national and international levels and corresponding to the elected administrative bodies. Community life centres largely around gatherings, observances, activities and events at the local level, although programmes are often arranged at the national and even the international level. The unity and interconnectedness of the international Baha'i community is such that Baha'is are often very well informed of activities that are taking place in other locations in their own country and elsewhere and, if they can afford it, will travel to participate in some of these. Baha'is describe themselves as members of particular national communities and pride themselves on being part of a single worldwide Baha'i community. However, on a daily basis, Baha'is generally identify most closely with their local community and when Baha'is refer to their 'community' they generally mean their local one.

Because the spiritual and social aspects of Baha'i life are integrated and are connected to personal transformations in the individual's life through the development of spiritual qualities, this needs to be reflected in one's social life in one's interactions with others. Thus the community also needs to reflect these qualities and to foster them in its members.

It is within the Baha'i community that the individual can learn the values, develop the attitudes and put into practice what he or she has learned in the home; equally, the values, attitudes and behaviours learned by interacting with other Baha'is in the community can be practised in the home, in the workplace and in other settings.

It is at the local community level that the individual learns and puts into practice a whole host of values, attitudes and behaviours which, Baha'is anticipate, hold the key to the transformation of world society. Thus, merely by attending a 19-day feast, for example, an individual is not only involved in Baha'i community life but is given the opportunity to learn how to consult and interact with people from different backgrounds and cultures, and is thereby facilitated in the struggle to abandon any prejudices he may have. He is involved in making decisions that affect himself and others, which compels him to adopt an outward-looking stance, and encourages him to broaden his vision even further and assists him in his efforts to become detached from any selfish ideas because he is obliged to think about others. These skills are useful at home (and can also be learned at home and brought to the Baha'i community) and in the workplace. At the same time, a body of people who have these skills is being created, not only in one location but in thousands around the world. It is the Baha'i experience that where there are significant numbers of such visionary and skilled communities, they have begun to influence their own neighbourhoods and towns socially and politically. Baha'is anticipate that as this process evolves, cities and even countries will be affected by such socially enlightened individuals and communities. Eventually, they suggest, such things as global trade and even global governance will be transformed because society will be imbued with these ideas and will be composed of significant numbers of people who think and act in accordance with them. Such people will eventually make up such a sizeable proportion of the population that they will become the drivers of political, social and economic decisions, which will then be made according to standards set by Baha'u'llah. While such a concept of the transformation of society may appear not only ambitious but impossible of achievement, it is an integral part of Baha'i belief and practice.

The Pattern of Baha'i Community Life

Baha'i communities are the focus of a variety of activities and events that touch every aspect of a Baha'i's life. In addition to the 19-day feasts and holy day commemorations arranged by the local assembly, there are three 'core' activities of community resource development – training institutes, devotional meetings and children's classes – which are often offered by individuals within the community, as well as 'deepening' or study classes and informal information events such as 'firesides'. Baha'i communities, as they gather strength and mature, also engage in a range of social and economic development activities that offer Baha'i strategies and principles to the solution of local issues or the betterment of the wider community.

The pattern of life of Baha'i communities is shaped by the Baha'i calendar. The Baha'i calendar, also called the Badi' calendar, was established by the Bab and approved by Baha'u'llah. Baha'u'llah set the beginning of the Baha'i era as 1844, the year of the declaration of the Bab.

The Baha'i calendar is based on the solar year of 365 days, five hours and about 50 minutes. Each year is divided into 19 months of 19 days each. Baha'u'llah specified that four intercalary days (five in a leap year), called Ayyam-i-Ha, should precede the 19th month.

New Year's Day (Naw-Ruz) falls on the spring equinox. This usually occurs on 21 March and at present Naw-Ruz is fixed on that day. However, in future, if the equinox takes place after sunset on 21 March, Naw-Ruz will be celebrated on 22 March.

The names of the Baha'i months were given by the Bab, who drew them from the 19 names of God invoked in a Shi'i prayer:

1	Baha	Splendour	21 March – 8 April
2	Jalal	Glory	9 April – 27 April
3	Jamal	Beauty	28 April – 16 May
4	'Azamat	Grandeur	17 May – 4 June
5	Nur	Light	5 June – 23 June
6	Rahmat	Mercy	24 June – 12 July
7	Kalimat	Words	13 July – 31 July
8	Kamal	Perfection	1 August – 19 August
9	Asma'	Names	20 August – 7 September
10	'Izzat	Might	8 September – 26 September
11	Mashiyyat	Will	27 September – 15 October
12	'Ilm	Knowledge	16 October – 3 November
13	Qudrat	Power	4 November – 22 November
14	Qawl	Speech	23 November – 11 December
15	Masa'il	Questions	12 December – 30 December
16	Sharaf	Honour	31 December – 18 January
17	Sultan	Sovereignty	19 January – 6 February
18	Mulk	Dominion	7 February – 25 February
19	'Ala'	Loftiness	2 March – 20 March

The days of the Baha'i week are:

1	Jalal	Glory	Saturday
2	Jamal	Beauty	Sunday
3	Kamal	Perfection	Monday
4	Fidal	Grace	Tuesday
5	'Idal	Justice	Wednesday
6	Istijlal	Majesty	Thursday
7	Istiqlal	Independence	Friday

Each of the days of the month is also given the name of one of the attributes of God. The names are the same as those of the 19 months; thus, Naw-Ruz, the first day of the first month, is called 'the day of Baha of the month of Baha'. If it fell on a Saturday, the first day of the Baha'i week, it would also be 'the day of Jalal'.

The Baha'i day of rest is Istiqlal (Friday) and the Baha'i day begins and ends at sunset.

19-Day Feast

On the first day of every Baha'i month Baha'is observe the 19-day feast and this forms the backdrop of community life. In the Kitab-i-Aqdas Baha'u'llah enjoined the Baha'is 'to offer a feast, once in every month, though only water be served; for God hath purposed to bind hearts together, albeit through both earthly and heavenly means' (Bahá'u'lláh, 1992, para. 57). 'Abdu'l-Baha added a devotional period to the basic social gathering and Shoghi Effendi included an administrative and consultative period, giving the final shape to the institution. Today, the 19-day feast is the principal gathering of Baha'is in a locality which all members of the Baha'i community, including children, and Baha'i visitors to the community are entitled to attend. Its intended purpose is to promote unity, ensure the progress of the Baha'i Faith and foster joy, and it is considered 'a vital medium for maintaining close and continued contact between the believers themselves, and also between them and the body of their elected representatives in the local community' (Shoghi Effendi, quoted in Universal House of Justice, 1989). Beyond this, the feast:

> links the individual to the collective processes by which a society is built or restored. Here, for instance, the Feast is an arena of democracy at the very root of society, where the Local Spiritual Assembly and the members of the community meet on common ground, where individuals are free to offer their gifts of thought, whether as new ideas or constructive criticism, to the building processes of an advancing civilization. Thus it can be seen that aside from its spiritual significance, this common institution of the people combines an array of elemental social disciplines which educate its participants in the essentials of responsible citizenship. (ibid.)

Participation in the feast is not obligatory but very important. In general, only Baha'is are permitted to attend the feast. The feast is held in an atmosphere of reverence, love and unity and addresses all the aspects of the individual and the community: the spiritual, intellectual, administrative and social.

The local spiritual assembly is responsible for calling the feast, arranging the devotional programme, fixing the agenda for consultation and providing refreshments. If a Baha'i community has a local Baha'i centre or haziratu'l-quds that is large enough, the feast will most likely be held there. At present, where Baha'i communities are small, the feast is often held in the home of a believer and it is customary for the host to select the prayers and readings for the devotional programme and to offer refreshments. In larger communities a committee may undertake these tasks on behalf of the local assembly.

The programme for the feast is in three parts: devotional, consultative and social. The devotional programme usually consists of readings and recitations primarily from the writings of Baha'u'llah, the Bab and 'Abdu'l-Baha or, occasionally, from the sacred scriptures of other

The World Order of Baha'u'llah encompasses all units of human society; integrates the spiritual, administrative and social processes of life; and canalises human expression in its varied forms towards the construction of a new civilization. The Nineteen Day Feast embraces all these aspects at the very base of society. Functioning in the village, the town, the city, it is an institution of which all the people of Bahá are members. It is intended to promote unity, ensure progress, and foster joy. (Universal House of Justice, 1989)

religions. There are no prayer leaders, designated readers or official reciters and Baha'u'llah did not specify how the devotional programme is to be conducted, leaving this to be decided by the local community. In many communities, believers take it in turn to read selected verses or they may be asked to choose appropriate ones themselves. In large communities a committee may choose the prayers and readers. Music may also be included, particularly the singing of prayers.

The second part of the feast is devoted to consultation on community business and issues, and the exchange of information between the institutions of the religion and the body of the Baha'is. One of the main functions of the feast is 'to enable individual believers to offer any suggestion to the Local Assembly which in its turn will pass it to the National Spiritual Assembly' (Shoghi Effendi, 1933b).

The social part of the feast is an integral part of the whole and the feast is not properly held without it. It is intended to be a period during which fellowship is fostered and the rich diversity of the Baha'i community can be explored. Refreshments are served, which may be as simple as glasses of water or as elaborate as complete meals. It is the time when community members can renew bonds of friendship, meet new people and exchange ideas and when children can consolidate their Baha'i identity. During this period, Baha'is usually talk among themselves, play music and listen to talks given by children and youth. Although the pattern for the 19-day feast is fixed, there is scope for infinite variety within this pattern to reflect the cultural diversity of the community, from music to the food served.

. . . the Feast is rooted in hospitality, with all its implications of friendliness, courtesy, service, generosity and conviviality. The very idea of hospitality as the sustaining spirit of so significant an institution introduces a revolutionary new attitude to the conduct of human affairs at all levels, an attitude which is critical to . . . world unity . . . It is in this divine festival that the foundation is laid for the realization of so unprecedented a reality. (Universal House of Justice, 1989)

Holy Days

Baha'is commemorate 11 holy days, which mark significant anniversaries of the central figures of the Baha'i Faith and important events and occasions. These are:

Festival of Naw-Ruz (Baha'i New Year)	21 March
Festival of Ridvan (Declaration of Baha'u'llah)	21 April – 2 May
Declaration of the Bab	23 May
Ascension of Baha'u'llah	29 May
Martyrdom of the Bab	9 July
Birth of the Bab	20 October
Birth of Baha'u'llah	12 November
Day of the Covenant	26 November
Ascension of 'Abdu'l-Baha	28 November

Baha'is do not work and children do not attend school on holy days, with the exception of the last two anniversaries which are associated with 'Abdu'l-Baha. During the Festival of Ridvan, work is suspended only on the first, ninth and twelfth days. Baha'is do not mark any anniversaries associated with Shoghi Effendi, nor are there any saint days.

There are no prescribed ceremonies for the commemoration of holy days. Many Baha'i communities hold devotional meetings or combine these with fellowship and appropriate social activities. Anyone, Baha'i or not, adult or child, is welcome to attend such commemorations.

Intercalary Days (Ayyam-i-Ha)

The four days (five in a leap year) before the last month of the Baha'i year are devoted to a spiritual preparation for the fast, hospitality, feasting, charity, gift-giving and visiting. While there are no prescribed activities, Baha'i families and communities often host parties during this period, visit each other, make special charitable donations, carry out acts of service to the wider community and give gifts to their children.

Training Institutes

In the 1990s the Universal House of Justice called for the establishment of training institutes in every country to 'endow ever-growing contingents of believers with the spiritual insights, the knowledge, and the skills needed to carry out the many tasks of accelerated expansion and consolidation' (*Training Institutes*, 1998). A primary task of the training institute is to provide a sequence of courses that will support and sustain the systematic development of human resources within the Baha'i community. Many countries have adopted the materials developed for this purpose over many years by the Ruhi Institute based in the Baha'i community of Colombia. The holding of training institute courses is one of the three core activities of every Baha'i community.

Devotional Meetings

One of the three core activities of Baha'i communities, devotional meetings are gatherings of Baha'is, their family and friends, often in their own homes, at which prayers and selections from the scriptures are read or recited. Music is frequently used in the programme and the room may be decorated with flowers or candles to provide a spiritually uplifting environment. Devotional meetings are open to everyone and are linked to the development of the Mashriqu'l-Adhkar (see below). There is no set programme or pattern for devotional meetings and they may be held as frequently as the hosts wish. All Baha'is and Baha'i families are encouraged to host regular devotional meetings if they are able and in many places people who are not themselves Baha'is host such meetings.

Children's Classes

The education of children is one of the highest priorities of the Baha'i community. It is generally recognised that one measure of the success of the Baha'i community is its ability to transmit the teachings of Baha'u'llah to successive generations. Thus, the Baha'i education of children is an important responsibility not only of the family but of the whole Baha'i community and its institutions and the holding of children's classes is one of the three core activities of Baha'i community development. Classes for the Baha'i education of children are open to all children and are taught by Baha'is, often youth or parents. The provision of classes varies from area to area. The classes generally introduce children to the Baha'i scriptures and focus on the development of spiritual qualities, habits and behaviours, as well as on Baha'i social teachings. Training of teachers for children's classes is provided, often through the training institute, and child protection requirements are strictly followed. Individual Baha'is, particularly youth, are encouraged to undertake the training necessary to become teachers.

Youth

The Baha'i Faith is often identified as a religion of young people. The forerunner of Baha'u'llah, the Bab, was only 25 when he proclaimed his mission and 31 when he was executed. Large numbers of converts to the religion, particularly in the 1960s and 1970s, have been from people under the age of 30.

Baha'is place much emphasis on the education and role of youth 'who can contribute so decisively to the virility, the purity, and the driving force of the life of the Baha'i community, and upon whom must depend the future orientation of its destiny, and the complete unfoldment of the potentialities with which God has endowed it' (Shoghi Effendi, 1990, p. 22). While not able to vote in Baha'i elections or serve on elected institutions until they reach the age of 21, Baha'i youth are appointed to committees and other agencies of the religion and form the backbone of its year of service programmes. It is while they are engaged in these services that young people further their knowledge of the values, attitudes, behaviours and skills that are required not only to administer the Baha'i community itself in the future but which also are so important to them in their work and as citizens.

Young people are described as the 'spearhead' of efforts to propagate the Baha'i Faith and to broaden its reach. They are at the forefront of the training institute process and are engaged in teaching children, offering service to others and hosting devotional meetings and firesides. They are encouraged to further their education, to become scholars of the Baha'i Faith and to train themselves in public speaking. At the same time, they are expected to uphold the same high standards of personal morality enjoined upon all Baha'is.

Baha'u'llah indicated that a person reaches spiritual maturity at the age of 15 and it is at this time that Baha'i young people take up their spiritual responsibilities such as fasting and obligatory prayer and are responsible for their own spiritual destiny. It is one of the duties of every local assembly to 'promote by every means in their power the material as well as the spiritual enlightenment of youth' (Shoghi Effendi, 1968, p. 38).

> Though lacking in experience and faced with insufficient resources, yet the adventurous spirit which they possess, and the vigour, the alertness, and optimism [Baha'i youth] have thus far so consistently shown, qualify them to play an active part in arousing the interest, and in securing the allegiance, of their fellow youth in those countries. No greater demonstration can be given to the peoples of both continents of the

youthful vitality and the vibrant power animating the life, and the institutions of the nascent Faith of Bahá'u'lláh than an intelligent, persistent, and effective participation of the Bahá'í youth, of every race, nationality, and class, in both the teaching and administrative spheres of Bahá'í activity. *(Shoghi Effendi, 1990, pp. 69–70)*

Year of Service

Baha'is have a high sense of service to others, seeing this as service to humanity as a whole and, ultimately, to God. Serving others and the community is a concrete way of applying the ideals outlined by Baha'u'llah to real situations and enables the individual to develop spiritual qualities of selflessness and detachment while offering practical assistance to those who need it. Children are educated to have a spirit of service and families and Baha'i communities often undertake regular service activities.

To provide channels for this, Baha'i communities have developed 'year of service' programmes whereby Baha'is, especially youth, may dedicate a part of their time to formal service projects. Often taken in a gap year between school and further education or before commencing employment, young people undertake such tasks as teaching children's classes, helping at orphanages and homes for the retired, providing administrative assistance to Baha'i communities, training other young people in music and dance skills, teaching literacy, running training institute programmes and generally doing whatever is required.

Women

> The world of humanity is possessed of two wings: the male and the female. So long as these two wings are not equivalent in strength, the bird will not fly. Until womankind reaches the same degree as man, until she enjoys the same arena of activity, extraordinary attainment for humanity will not be realised; humanity cannot wing its way to heights of real attainment.
> ('Abdu'l-Bahá, 1982, p. 375)

The Baha'i Faith recognises that for most of the history of humankind women have been disadvantaged: they have not had access to education; there has generally been a lower investment in them; their skills and insights have not been highly valued or rewarded and they lack legal protection. Traditional thinking about the role of women has often left them in a very weakened position, especially when young or widowed, and vulnerable to physical and other abuses. In some parts of the world they are required to undergo painful and degrading practices such as genital mutilation. They have, by and large, borne the burden of parenthood and domestic responsibilities unaided and, to this day, in many societies are unable to get credit to purchase their own homes or are not entitled to inherit from male relatives. Even in so-called advanced societies there remains a perception that women are not really cut out for 'life at the top', whatever that may mean for a particular society, so even though there may be legal structures in place, they often earn less than their male counterparts and are less likely to rise in their professions to the same heights as men.

Baha'is seek to change these attitudes at every level – in individual families, in the community, at work, at government level, at the international level. Baha'is are particularly concerned with the education of girls as a way forward but also for older women and aged women. The main principles that drive the Baha'i position are the recognition of the oneness of humanity; the equality of women and men, without which there can be no peace in the world; the need to promote the advancement of women, without which there can be no social stability, justice or prosperity; a recasting of the importance of mothers and families in general; the need for partnership between women and men in all fields of endeavour; and the belief that men can change and will change.

Underpinning these principles and values are important behaviours. For example, girls get priority of education over boys when a family cannot afford to educate all its children, and women themselves are expected to participate in community affairs, in decision-making and governance. It was 'Abdu'l-Baha, during his travels in Europe and North America between 1911 and 1913, who articulated the Baha'i teachings about the equality of women with men and the benefits of the advance of women. In a discussion with a suffragette in London in 1911, he set out the Baha'i position on the participation of women in decision-making and governance: 'The woman has greater moral courage than the man; she has also special gifts which enable her to govern in moments of danger and crisis' ('Abdu'l-Bahá in London, 1982, p. 103).

To promote these ideas Baha'is work not only within their own communities to establish equality between women and men but also with other organisations such as UNIFEM and UNICEF, and they support the Beijing Platform for Action. However, Baha'is recognise that the best way to promulgate these ideas is to apply them to the Baha'i community itself and to offer the Baha'i community as a model for others. Thus Baha'i women are encouraged to 'become proficient in the arts and sciences', to enter the fields of 'industrial and agricultural sciences' ('Abdu'l-Bahá, 1982, p. 283) and to take an active role in the life of their Baha'i communities. Baha'is seek to advance the leadership and responsibility of women by developing their consultation skills – formally through training days and traditional media (in conjunction with UNIFEM) and informally through practice on Baha'i institutions and 19-day feast; and by providing education for girls, particularly, through non-formal education projects, including tutorial schools, literacy centres and pre-schools – there are about one thousand such centres in the world now, more than 50 per cent of which are in Asia and the Pacific. Baha'is seek to raise the status of mothers by educating men to understand their role and by offering women training in life skills, especially literacy, nutrition, hygiene, first aid and so on; by promoting wealth creation schemes, including microfinance projects and crafts; by working with other agencies to reduce violence against women, especially within families; by using traditional media to focus on the undesirability of genital mutilation, with the aim of eliminating the practice; and by providing education in money management for both women and men. Baha'i projects to advance women exist in most countries where Baha'i communities function – over 170 to date.

The Baha'i attitude towards women and their contribution to world peace is perhaps best summarised by the Universal House of Justice:

> The emancipation of women, the achievement of full equality between the sexes, is one of the most important, though less acknowledged prerequisites of peace. The denial of such equality perpetrates an injustice against one half of the world's population and promotes in men harmful attitudes and habits that are carried from the family to the workplace, to political life, and ultimately to international relations. There are no grounds, moral, practical, or biological, upon which such denial can be justified. Only as women are welcomed into full partnership in all fields of human endeavour will the moral and psychological climate be created in which international peace can emerge. *(Universal House of Justice, 1985)*

Scholarship

Baha'u'llah encouraged the spirit of inquiry, 'the first principle of Baha'u'llah', according to 'Abdu'l-Baha, being the 'independent investigation of truth' (*Japan Will Turn Ablaze*, p. 35). In the writings of 'Abdu-'l-Baha and Shoghi Effendi this concept of searching for truth for oneself is linked to the recognition of the oneness of humanity and the establishment of peace, as it enables humanity to cease continually repeating the mistakes of the past. Connected to this is the concept that religion and science are two ways of considering the same reality and that they should therefore complement each other, hence it is important that both be researched and applied to the uplifting of humanity. Thus providing children and young people with a broad education that includes the study of scientific subjects and the arts is promoted by Baha'is.

The study of the Baha'i teachings, history and laws is the responsibility of each individual. A major function of Baha'i scholarship is to apply the teachings of the Faith to contemporary problems. It is recognised that some would wish to go beyond this and to study the history and teachings of the religion at a deeper level, and the Baha'i community provides for this. For example, the Association for Baha'i Studies has been established to cultivate the formal study of the religion and to create opportunities for the presentation of the Baha'i teachings in universities and institutions of higher education.

Baha'i Seasonal Schools

To enable people to learn more about the Baha'i Faith and to fulfil their need to study its teachings more deeply than they can do alone, many national communities provide schools or educational centres for Baha'is, their families, friends and other interested persons. Some national communities have permanent facilities which are open more or less all year and offer libraries, Internet access and residential accommodation. Other countries may rent such accommodation and offer a Baha'i school lasting a week or so, often during holiday seasons. Residential schools provide an opportunity for Baha'is to live together for a short time in accordance with Baha'i ideals.

A variety of subjects may be studied at such schools, including aspects of Baha'i history, Baha'i social and spiritual teachings and practices, Baha'i administration and Baha'i law. Training institute programmes or teacher training classes may also be provided. Increasingly, the arts play a significant role, both as an educational tool and as a subject of study, as well as providing entertainment and a cultural dimension. Adults, children and youth generally have separate but integrated programmes. Shoghi Effendi has said that these schools will develop into the universities of the future.

Where Baha'i communities are mature enough and there is a need, they develop schools providing a general education to all children, based on the educational requirements set out by the government but implementing Baha'i values and principles. Universities inspired by the Baha'i teachings have been opened in a few countries.

Baha'i Houses of Worship (Mashriqu'l-Adhkar)

In his Most Holy Book Baha'u'llah established the centre of a community's spiritual and social life as the Mashriqu'l-Adhkar ('dawning-place of the praises or remembrances or mention of God'):

> Blessed is he who, at the hour of dawn, centring his thoughts on God, occupied with His remembrance, and supplicating His forgiveness, directeth his steps to the Mashriqu'l-Adhkár and, entering therein, seateth himself in silence to listen to the verses of God, the Sovereign, the Mighty, the All-Praised. Say: The Mashriqu'l-Adhkár is each and every building which hath been erected in cities and villages for the celebration of My praise. Such is the name by which it hath been designated before the throne of glory, were ye of those who understand. *(Bahá'u'lláh, 1992, para. 115)*

The term Mashriqu'l-Adhkar refers to a variety of related spiritual and humanitarian institutions and activities. It primarily refers to the cluster of buildings and institutions devoted to the spiritual and social well-being of the community and to its education and scientific training, including a central house of worship, a university, a travellers' hospice, a hospital and drug dispensary, a school for orphans and a home for the infirm (ibid. Notes, p. 190). It is also used to refer to the house of worship itself, the 'central edifice' which is the 'spiritual heart of the community' (Universal House of Justice, 1984a). Further, the term is used to refer to 'any building or room which is reserved for devotions; devotional meetings, particularly dawn prayers; and the heart of the sincere worshipper' (Momen, 1989, pp. 149–50).

At present there are only seven houses of worship, or temples – one on each continent and one in Samoa – and an eighth is being built in Chile. The first house of worship, in Russian Turkmenistan, was damaged by an earthquake and was demolished. Only a few of the institutions that are to surround the house of worship have been developed. Houses of worship are open to all people and, like all Baha'i institutions and activities, are designed to foster unity. 'Abdu'l-Baha developed this theme when in 1912 he laid the foundation stone of the house of worship built near Chicago:

the original purpose of temples and houses of worship is simply that of unity – places of meeting where various peoples, different races and souls of every capacity may come together in order that love and agreement should be manifest between them . . . that all religions, races and sects may come together within its universal shelter. *('Abdu'l-Bahá, 1982, p. 65)*

'Abdu'l-Baha indicated that the house of worship should be circular in shape, have nine sides, and be surrounded by nine gardens with paths (ibid. p. 71), and Shoghi Effendi added that they should be 'graceful in outline' with a 'delicate architectural beauty' (Shoghi Effendi, 1982, pp. 245–6). Although all the houses of worship built so far have domes and nine doors, these are not required.

The house of worship is a place for prayer, the reading and singing of scriptures, meditation and quiet reflection. No other activities are to take place there, a prohibition that includes sermons, weddings and funeral services. No musical instruments are played there, but a cappella singing of the scriptures is encouraged. The prayers offered at the house of worship are to be reflected in service to humanity, as provided in the humanitarian institutions surrounding it. Baha'is anticipate that in the future, when each local community has its own Mashriqu'l-Adhkar, one of the features of community life will be the gathering of people each day between dawn and two hours after sunrise to pray together before beginning the day's work and activities.

Baha'i Centres (Haziratu'l-Quds)

The administrative headquarters of a national Baha'i community are, in general, situated at a national Baha'i centre or *haziratu'l-quds* ('sacred fold'). It is the seat of the national spiritual assembly and where the secretariat is located. In addition to its administrative functions, it 'should include such activities of a social and intellectual character, both local and national, as can best establish its character as the foremost teaching and administrative centre of the Faith' in the country' (*Directives from the Guardian*, p. 36).

A local community that is large enough may have a local Baha'i centre as the seat of the local spiritual assembly, fulfilling the same purpose at the local level as the national one. Baha'i centres are also used for the holding of community activities, such as 19-day feasts, holy days, children's classes, devotional meetings, study circles and youth activities, and may be used for weddings and funerals.

Baha'i Funds

The activities of the Baha'i Faith are paid for by the voluntary contributions of the Baha'is themselves. One of the distinguishing features of the religion is that only Baha'is may contribute to its funds, as contributing is considered a 'spiritual privilege, not open to those who have not accepted Baha'u'llah', a 'responsibility and a source of bounty'. Baha'is consider that giving to the Baha'i funds will 'attract the confirmations of God and enhance the dignity and self-respect of the individuals and the community' (Universal House of Justice, 1985d).

The amount to be contributed is not fixed, nor is it significant. For Baha'is, the important thing is the degree of sacrifice of the donor, the love with which he or she makes the contribution and the unity of the Baha'is in contributing (ibid.)

There are several Baha'i funds. Each local spiritual assembly will have a fund to support its own work, as will every national spiritual assembly. A continental fund supports the work of the Continental Boards of Counsellors, the Auxiliary Board members and their assistants, while the International Fund, administered by the Universal House of Justice, supports Baha'i work at the international level. The World Centre Endowment Fund pays for the upkeep of the Baha'i shrines in the Holy Land and the buildings and gardens on Mount Carmel. There are also funds for various projects, such as the building of a new Baha'i centre locally or nationally, the building of a new house of worship and for sponsoring travelling teachers or pioneers. Baha'is are encouraged to support each fund personally.

Huququ'llah (The Right of God)

Baha'is believe that everything that exists has been created by God and, in reality, belongs to Him. In acknowledgement of this, Baha'is offer back to God a portion of the value of their possessions as a spiritual obligation and bounty. By doing so, Baha'u'llah has indicated that one's remaining wealth and possessions are purified and may be used for any purpose one wishes.

This offering back to God of a portion of one's wealth is known as 'the Right of God', Huququ'llah. Baha'u'llah set out the provision of this law in the Kitab-i-Aqdas. Briefly, Baha'is offer to the head of the religion, today the Universal House of Justice, 19 per cent of the increase in their liquid wealth from the time of the last payment. Certain categories of possessions, such as one's home and those things that are 'needful', are exempt from the payment of Huquq. It is left to the individual to decide which of his possessions are needful.

Payment of Huquq is an obligation but payment must be made in the right spirit – 'the spirit of joy, fellowship and contentment' (Bahá-'u'lláh, in *Compilation*, 1991, vol. 1, p. 490). Baha'is are not forced to pay Huquq – and should not be made to feel that they are being forced – and no one is ever solicited to pay, although each Board of Trustees for Huquq provides guidance on how calculations and pay-ments can be made and offers educational programmes.

The payment of Huquq is different from making contributions to the Baha'i funds. From the Baha'i perspective, the Huququ'llah already belongs to God while voluntary contributions are made from what belongs to the individual.

Baha'u'llah designated those to whom the head of the religion is to disburse the money raised by the Huquq: the poor, the disabled, the needy and orphans, as well as meeting the essential needs of the Baha'i Faith itself. The payment of Huquq is not merely an economic exer-cise. Bahá'ís consider it a spiritual responsibility and privilege that will bring benefits to the donor, as well as to the wider community.

Propagation of the Baha'i Faith

Baha'u'llah enjoined his followers to teach his faith. For Baha'is, teaching the religion to others is the greatest of all God's gifts and is the personal responsibility of every Baha'i.

The Baha'i Faith is largely spread by word of mouth and by the example of the Baha'is themselves. Teaching is to be undertaken in a spirit of kindliness and goodwill and to be carried out with wisdom and humility, as a servant offering a gift to a king. A Baha'i teacher is to be 'imbued with praiseworthy attributes and divine qualities' ('Abdu'l-Bahá, 1930, p. 19). Baha'i parents are to teach the religion to their children in the same spirit as they teach others.

There are no set ways to teach. Many Baha'is open their homes for informal 'firesides' or introductory information meetings for people wishing to learn about the Baha'i Faith, at which hospitality is offered, some aspect of the religion is discussed and questions are answered. Such teaching in one's own home was recommended by Shoghi Effendi, who advised that firesides should be held at least once every 19 days. Baha'is are encouraged to teach their families, friends, work-mates and like-minded individuals, but they are not allowed to pros-elytise, dispute with anyone or use any form of coercion.

Increasingly, friends and families of Baha'is are attending the training institute programmes, particularly the Ruhi Institute's *Reflec-tions on the Life of the Spirit*, and this has proved to be a useful way to introduce the Baha'i spiritual concepts to many people. Others bring their children to children's classes or attend devotional meetings and hence a large 'community of interest' has grown up around the Baha'i community itself from which many new Baha'is are drawn.

There are no 'professional' Baha'i teachers, although many people do devote significant portions of their lives to telling others about the religion and sharing its message, sometimes moving – 'pioneering' – to another town or even another country to do so. Any Baha'i may become a pioneer and, in general, there are no special requirements, although certain places may need specific skills, such as a language. At the international level, the Universal House of Justice, in consultation with national spiritual assemblies and the International Teaching Centre, determines where pioneers are needed and asks different national communities to provide them. At the national and local level, a pioneer is a Baha'i who settles in another place within the country with the purpose of teaching the religion.

There are no missionaries in the usual sense of the term. In general, pioneers settle in an area, establish a home, begin work, and live and teach the Baha'i Faith as they would anywhere. Sometimes it is very difficult for pioneers to obtain work and then some of their living expenses may be defrayed by the Baha'i funds. This is decided on a case by case basis.

Similarly, Baha'is who travel with the purpose of teaching the religion are known as travelling teachers. As with pioneers, any Baha'i may become a travelling teacher and there are no special requirements or training programmes. Many Baha'is travel and teach for short periods of a week or two in their holidays. Travelling teachers generally support themselves but occasionally funding is available for particular projects. Baha'is often arrange their own programmes, but many national communities have committees that will assist if a teacher is going abroad.

8

History

The history of the Baha'i Faith revolves around four main figures. By far the most important of these is Baha'u'llah, upon whose teachings the religion is based. His forerunner, the Bab, established an independent religion, the Babi religion, but also prophesied that he was merely preparing the way for a much more important figure that was to come. Baha'u'llah appointed his son 'Abdu'l-Baha to be his successor and the authorised interpreter of his teachings. 'Abdu'l-Baha in turn appointed Shoghi Effendi as his successor and also as the authorised interpreter of the Baha'i teachings.

The Bab (1819–1850)

The Bab put forward his claim in 1844 in the city of Shiraz in the south of Persia (Iran). Having instructed his first 18 disciples, the Letters of the Living, to disperse throughout the region and proclaim his message, the Bab set off for Mecca where he proclaimed his mission at the heart of the Islamic world in the midst of the pilgrimage season. His claim aroused fierce opposition among the Islamic religious leaders in Iran and Iraq. The foremost religious leaders of both the Sunni and Shi'i sect of Islam gathered in Baghdad and issued a joint declaration condemning the new teaching. Despite this, the teaching was spread throughout Iran, Iraq and into India by the Letters of the Living, attracting many thousands of people including many of the ulama, the Islamic clerical class. Among the Letters of the Living was a woman, Tahirih, who, despite the disadvantage of her sex, was able to proclaim the message of the Bab in Iraq and convert many, including members of the ulama.

Although the Bab was arrested on his return from Mecca and received harsh treatment at the hands of the governor of Shiraz, he conducted himself with such dignity that many of the people of the town were won over. Then in 1846 the Bab left Shiraz and proceeded north to the city of Isfahan. Here the governor was friendly and the Bab was accommodated at the home of one of the leading religious figures of the city. The king of Iran, Muhammad Shah, had by now heard of the stir that the Bab was causing and expressed a desire to meet him. His prime minister, however, Haji Mirza Aqasi, feared that if the Bab met the Shah, his own position and influence over the Shah would be threatened. He therefore did all in his power to prevent the two from meeting. In the event, the governor of Isfahan died in early 1847 and the prime minister ordered the Bab to be imprisoned in a fortress in the remote north-west region of Iran. He hoped in this way to isolate the Bab and erase his influence.

The followers of the Bab were not deterred, however, and many of them travelled to the fortress. The warden of the fortress was soon won over and allowed them access to the Bab. Seeing his plan thwarted, in 1848 the prime minister moved the Bab to another remote fortress, also in north-west Iran, but this imprisonment was no more successful in isolating the Bab. Eventually, the prime minister decided to have the Bab brought to Tabriz, the capital of the north-west province of Iran, and put on trial there before the crown prince, Nasiru'd-Din; he hoped to intimidate and humiliate the Bab by having him interrogated by a number of prominent religious leaders. The trial, however, gave the Bab the opportunity to proclaim openly his claim to be the Mahdi, the Promised Saviour of all Islam.

Tahirih, who had been expelled from Iraq as a result of her successful propagation of the message of the Bab, was attacked in her home town of Qazvin and fled to Tehran. From here she proceeded to a place called Badasht, on the road from Tehran to the north-west of the country, to which the Bab had summoned all the Letters of the Living and his other followers. At this conference, which occurred at almost the same time as the Bab's trial in Tabriz, the fact that the Bab had inaugurated a new religious dispensation was openly proclaimed and the abrogation of the laws of Islam was symbolised by the fact that Tahirih appeared before the gathering without a veil, which was required by Islamic law.

In September 1848 Muhammad Shah died and the crown prince who had presided over the trial of the Bab in Tabriz now became Nasiru'd-Din Shah. Haji Mirza Aqasi was deposed as prime minister and Mirza Taqi Khan was installed. But the change brought no benefit to the Bab, and in fact it made the situation worse. The new prime minister began a campaign against the Bab and his followers. When a group of Babis was attacked in the northern province of Mazandaran and surrounded at the shrine of Shaykh Tabarsi at the instigation of a local religious leader, the prime minister sent troops from the royal army against them. The siege lasted seven months and between 400 and 600 Babis were surrounded in a place with no natural fortifications by some ten to twelve thousand royal troops with

> The Bab's passionate sincerity could not be doubted, for he had given his life for his faith. And that there must be something in his message that appealed to men and satisfied their souls was witnessed to by the fact that thousands gave their lives in his cause and millions now follow him. If a young man could, in only six years of ministry, by the sincerity of his purpose and the attraction of his personality, so inspire rich and poor, cultured and illiterate, alike, with belief in himself and his doctrines that they would remain staunch though hunted down and without trial sentenced to death, sawn asunder, strangled, shot, blown from guns; and if men of high position and culture in Persia, Turkey and Egypt in numbers to this day adhere to his doctrines; his life must be one of those events in the last hundred years which is really worth study. (Younghusband, 1923, p. 184)

cannons. Despite the overwhelming advantage that the royal forces had, they were unable to overcome the Babis who were led by two of the Letters of the Living. Eventually, the royal prince who was leading the Shah's army was forced to resort to deception and trickery. He swore on the Qur'an that he would give safe passage to the Babis who were by now starving, having been cut off from all food. Then, when the Babis emerged from behind the fortifications they had constructed, the royal army fell upon them and massacred them.

The Shaykh Tabarsi upheaval was followed by further similar episodes. In the southern town of Nayriz in the south of Iran, not far from Shiraz, Vahid, a cleric of national importance. had become a Babi. He was attacked by the governor of the town and the governor of Shiraz sent troops against the Babis. Again the siege of the Babis ended in treachery with the Babis being promised an amnesty and then being massacred when they emerged from their positions. In the town of Zanjan on the road between Tehran and Tabriz, one of the local religious leaders, Hujjat, became a Babi and was attacked by the other religious leaders. Again, royal troops were summoned against the Babis and the ensuing conflict lasted eight months until the Babis were eventually overcome.

These large-scale episodes involving hundreds of Babis and thousands of royal troops were accompanied by numerous other smaller episodes all around the country. Eventually the prime minister decided that the best way to put an end to the upheaval would be to kill the Bab. He gave instructions for the Bab to be taken to Tabriz and executed. In the event even this became a source of fame for the Bab, since, as was attested even by the British ambassador to Iran, when the smoke cleared after the firing squad fired for the first time, the Bab had disappeared. He was found completing some dictation to his secretary. He was brought before another firing squad, which this time succeeded in executing him.

Baha'u'llah (1817–1892)

Baha'u'llah was born in Tehran, the capital of Persia, which is situated a little to the north of the centre of the country. He was the son of a high government official and was raised in luxury. But when he heard the message of the Bab, he immediately accepted it and became one of the main coordinators of the Babis. His home in Tehran became a centre of Babi activity and he was the organiser of the Badasht conference. As a result of these activities, Baha'u'llah became the focus of persecution and he gradually lost all of his position and wealth.

In 1852 an event occurred that was to have profound consequences for Baha'u'llah and all of the Babis. A small group of Babis made an attempt on the life of the Shah, seeking revenge for the execution of the Bab. The attempt was poorly planned and failed, but the consequences were serious. The Shah ordered a general massacre of the Babis. Baha'u'llah, although he had had nothing to do with the attempted assassination, was arrested and kept in an underground prison for four months.

During this imprisonment, Baha'u'llah had an experience which he regards as the beginning of his mission. He describes it as a vision of a heavenly Maiden suspended in the air, addressing all in heaven and earth, and proclaiming Baha'u'llah to be the Best-Beloved of the worlds and the Cause of God. Upon his release, Baha'u'llah was ordered into exile. Turning down an offer of asylum from the Russian ambassador, Baha'u'llah chose to go to Baghdad which was at that time a provincial capital in the Ottoman Empire. Here he gradually emerged as the leader of the Babi community. This community had become completely demoralised and driven underground by the persecutions of the previous years. Baha'u'llah sent a stream of writings and emissaries to the Babis of Iran, gradually reviving them. He faced opposition, however, from his half-brother Azal, who claimed leadership of the Babi community.

Among the books produced by Baha'u'llah during this period was the Kitab-i-Iqan in which he lays down the fundamental principles for the understanding of scripture and also describes the progressive and continuing nature of God's guidance to humanity through the founders of the religions of the world. Another work was the Hidden Words, a series of short statements relating to spiritual and ethical themes. Also relating to this period is the Seven Valleys, Baha'u'llah's foremost mystical work.

Eventually, the revival of the Babi community caused the Persian government to demand the removal of Baha'u'llah from so close to their borders. The Ottoman government asked Baha'u'llah to come to the capital Istanbul. Just before leaving, Baha'u'llah announced to the Babis in his company that he was the one whose coming had been prophesied by the Bab. This announcement occurred in the Garden of Ridvan, an event that is commemorated by Baha'is as the most holy of their festivals.

After three months in Istanbul, Baha'u'llah was exiled in the severest winter weather to Edirne, in what is now European Turkey, arriving there in December 1863. He lived in this town for five years. During this time the rupture between Baha'u'llah and his half-brother Azal became complete after the latter tried to poison him. Also during these years Baha'u'llah initiated a series of letters to the kings and rulers of the world in which he put forward his claim to be the promised one of all the religions of the world. In his letter to Queen Victoria, Baha'u'llah commends her for stopping the slave trade and for extending democracy.

In 1868, as a result of false accusations made by Azal and the general insecurity of the Ottomans about their European provinces, Baha'u'llah was exiled to 'Akka in what was then the Ottoman province of Syria and is now the state of Israel. At first he was imprisoned in the citadel of the town but he was later placed under house arrest in a house in the town. In 1873 he wrote his most important book, the Kitab-i-Aqdas, his book of laws.

Baha'u'llah moved outside the walls of 'Akka in 1877, finally settling in the mansion of Bahji, a few miles north of 'Akka, where he was to remain until his passing in 1892. In this period he wrote a number of works giving the social teachings of his religion. His shrine at Bahji is the holiest place on earth for Baha'is. By the time of the passing of Baha'u'llah, the Baha'i Faith had spread to Egypt, Syria, Anatolia, the Caucasus, Central Asia and India.

Throughout his life Baha'u'llah experienced the sufferings that many of the poor in the world endure today. He and his family endured poor water supplies, overcrowding in the homes they were assigned, lack of sanitary conditions, the unavailability of fresh food, lack of employment and ineffective government. Baha'u'llah and his family were also prisoners and refugees, victims of prejudice, disinformation, lack of concern for others and fear. Stones were thrown at the children of the family by those whose hatred of the Babis and Baha'is

My conductor paused for a moment while I removed my shoes. Then, with a quick movement of the hand, he withdrew, and, as I passed replaced the curtain; and I found myself in a large apartment, along the upper end of which ran a low divan, while on the side opposite to the door were placed two or three chairs. Though I dimly suspected whither I was going and whom I was to behold (for no distinct intimation had been given to me), a second or two elapsed ere, with a throb of wonder and awe, I became definitely conscious that the room was not untenanted. In the corner where the divan met the wall sat a wondrous and venerable figure, crowned with a felt head-dress of the kind called taj by dervishes (but of unusual height and make), round the base of which was wound a small white turban. The face of him on whom I gazed I can never forget, though I cannot describe it. Those piercing eyes seemed to read one's very soul; power and authority sat on that ample brow; while the deep lines on the forehead and face implied an age which the jet-black hair and beard flowing down in indistinguishable luxuriance almost to the waist seemed to belie. No need to ask in whose presence I stood, as I bowed myself before one who is the object of a devotion and love which kings might envy and emperors sigh for in vain!

A mild dignified voice bade me be seated, and then continued: – 'Praise be to God that thou hast attained! . . . Thou hast come to see a prisoner and an exile . . . We desire but the good of the world and the happiness of the nations; yet they deem us a stirrer up of strife and sedition worthy of bondage and banishment . . . That all nations should become one in faith and all men as brothers; that the bonds of affection and unity between the sons of men should be strengthened; that diversity of religion should cease and differences of race be annulled – what harm is there in this? . . .

Yet so it shall be; these fruitless strifes, these ruinous wars shall pass away, and the 'Most Great Peace' shall come . . . Do not you in Europe need this also? Is not this that which Christ foretold? . . . Yet do we see your kings and rulers lavishing their treasures more freely on means for the destruction of the human race than on that which would conduce to the happiness of mankind . . . These strifes and this bloodshed and discord must cease, and all men be as one kindred and one family . . . Let not a man glory in this, that he loves his country; let him rather glory in this, that he loves his kind. (Interview by Professor E. G. Browne of Cambridge University with Baha'u'llah, cited in 'Abdu'l-Baha, *Traveller's Narrative*, 1891, vol. 2, pp. xxxix–xl) had been aroused by others who were ignorant and feared them. Baha'u'llah, his family and many Baha'is were the victims of injustice, arbitrary and corrupt government and abuses of their human rights. Baha'u'llah himself was falsely accused, beaten and deprived of his property unjustly. When, therefore, Baha'u'llah writes of the need for social justice, the eradication of poverty, the prevention of forced migration, the need for clean water in which to wash, the education of mothers and girl children, the requirement of a high moral standard for leaders, the application of ethical principles to business and the upholding of the rule of law, he is writing of things which he experienced at first hand and about which he cared deeply.

'Abdu'l-Baha (1844–1921)

In the Book of My Covenant, Baha'u'llah's will, he appointed his eldest son, 'Abdu'l-Baha, as his successor. 'Abdu'l-Baha became thus the centre of a covenant that Baha'u'llah established with his followers that they would turn to 'Abdu'l-Baha to resolve any questions or disputes that arose among them. 'Abdu'l-Baha is also the perfect exemplar of the Baha'i teachings. Just as Baha'u'llah had been opposed by his half-brother, so 'Abdu'l-Baha was also opposed by his half-brother. Despite the fact that a number of leading Baha'is deserted 'Abdu'l-Baha when he succeeded his father, the over-whelming majority of Baha'is remained loyal to him.

In 1894 an important development occurred with the spread of the Baha'i teachings to North America. From here the Baha'i Faith spread to Europe and across the Pacific to Hawaii, Japan and Australia. When 'Abdu'l-Baha was freed from the restrictions imposed upon him by the terms of his exile, he travelled to Europe and North America in 1911 to 1913, visiting the newly formed Baha'i communities and speaking at societies, churches and private meetings wherever he went. His journeys gave a great impetus to the development of the Baha'i communities in these areas.

'Abdu'l-Baha kept up a stream of correspondence throughout his lifetime, mainly with individual Baha'is. Among his more important writings are *The Secret of Divine Civilization*, in which he gives a blueprint for the social and economic development of a nation; *A Traveller's Narrative*, which is a history of the Baha'i Faith; and the *Tablets of the Divine Plan*, in which he charts the future spread of the Baha'i Faith. Many of his talks were also published.

Shoghi Effendi (1897–1957)

When 'Abdu'l-Baha passed away in 1921 he left a Will and Testament in which he appointed his grandson Shoghi Effendi to be the Guardian of the Baha'i Faith, a position that included being the authoritative interpreter of the Baha'i scriptures. Shoghi Effendi spent the first 15 years of his ministry setting up the Baha'i administration and ensuring its proper functioning according to spiritual principles. Local spiritual assemblies and national spiritual assemblies were erected wherever there were Baha'i communities.

Once the Baha'i administration was in place in those countries that had substantial Baha'i communities, Shoghi Effendi began to implement a series of plans to spread the Baha'i Faith to all those parts of the world where it did not yet exist. At first plans were given to individual Baha'i communities; then in 1952, he launched a global plan. This plan met with a great deal of success and led to the first signs of the enrolment of large numbers of Baha'is. Shoghi Effendi passed away in 1957 and there was an interregnum during which the administration of the Baha'i Faith was left in the hands of a number of individuals called 'Hands of the Cause of God'.

The Universal House of Justice

In 1963 it was finally possible for some 56 national spiritual assemblies from around the world to elect the Universal House of Justice, an institution ordained in the writings of Baha'u'llah as the supreme authority in the Baha'i Faith. This body began by continuing Shoghi Effendi's planned expansion of the Baha'i Faith. In recent years it has also made the development of Baha'i community life a priority for the Baha'i world, through the institution of three core activities which each Baha'i community should try to establish: devotional programmes, study circles and children's classes.

Notes

1. In the remainder of this stirring passage Baha'u'llah goes on to explain how exalted God is above the comprehension of His creation:

> The conceptions of the devoutest of mystics, the attainments of the most accomplished amongst men, the highest praise which human tongue or pen can render are all the product of man's finite mind and are conditioned by its limitations. Ten thousand Prophets, each a Moses, are thunderstruck upon the Sinai of their search at His forbidding voice, 'Thou shalt never behold Me!'; whilst a myriad Messengers, each as great as Jesus, stand dismayed upon their heavenly thrones by the interdiction, 'Mine Essence thou shalt never apprehend!' From time immemorial He hath been veiled in the ineffable sanctity of His exalted Self, and will everlastingly continue to be wrapt in the impenetrable mystery of His unknowable Essence. Every attempt to attain to an understanding of His inaccessible Reality hath ended in complete bewilderment, and every effort to approach His exalted Self and envisage His Essence hath resulted in hopelessness and failure.
>
> How bewildering to me, insignificant as I am, is the attempt to fathom the sacred depths of Thy knowledge! How futile my efforts to visualize the magnitude of the power inherent in Thine handiwork - the revelation of Thy creative power! How can mine eye, which hath no faculty to perceive itself, claim to have discerned Thine Essence, and how can mine heart, already powerless to apprehend the significance of its own potentialities, pretend to have comprehended Thy nature? How can I claim to have known Thee, when the entire creation is bewildered by Thy mystery, and how can I confess not to have known Thee, when, lo, the whole universe proclaimeth Thy Presence and testifieth to Thy truth? The portals of Thy grace have throughout eternity been open, and the means of access unto Thy Presence made available, unto all created things, and the revelations of Thy matchless Beauty have at all times been imprinted upon the realities of all beings, visible and invisible. Yet, notwithstanding this most gracious favour, this perfect and consummate bestowal, I am moved to testify that Thy court of holiness and glory is immeasurably exalted above the knowledge of all else besides Thee, and the mystery of Thy Presence is inscrutable to every mind except Thine own. No one except Thyself can unravel the secret of Thy nature, and naught else but Thy

transcendental Essence can grasp the reality of Thy unsearchable being. How vast the number of those heavenly and all-glorious beings who, in the wilderness of their separation from Thee, have wandered all the days of their lives, and failed in the end to find Thee! How great the multitude of the sanctified and immortal souls who were lost and bewildered while seeking in the desert of search to behold Thy face! Myriad are Thine ardent lovers whom the consuming flame of remoteness from Thee hath caused to sink and perish, and numberless are the faithful souls who have willingly laid down their lives in the hope of gazing on the light of Thy countenance. The sighs and moans of these longing hearts that pant after Thee can never reach Thy holy court, neither can the lamentations of the wayfarers that thirst to appear before Thy face attain Thy seat of glory. (Bahá'u'lláh, 1983, pp. 62–4)

2. 'O people of the earth! Living in seclusion or practising asceticism is not acceptable in the presence of God' (Bahá'u'lláh, 1988b, p. 71). 'O concourse of monks! Seclude not yourselves in your churches and cloisters. Come ye out of them by My leave, and busy, then, yourselves with what will profit you and others. Thus commandeth you He Who is the Lord of the Day of Reckoning' (Bahá'u'lláh, 1988a, p. 49).

3. 'O people of Bahá! It is incumbent upon each one of you to engage in some occupation – such as a craft, a trade or the like. We have exalted your engagement in such work to the rank of worship of the one true God' (Bahá'u'lláh, 1991; para. 33).

4. It is interesting to note that 'Abdu'l-Baha was describing his own home, in which he was a prisoner of the Ottoman Turks from 1868 until 1908.

5. 'Say: Teach ye the Cause of God, O people of Bahá, for God hath prescribed unto every one the duty of proclaiming His Message, and regardeth it as the most meritorious of all deeds' (Bahá'u'lláh, 1983, p. 278).

Timeline of Important Events

1817:	Birth of Baha'u'llah in Tehran, Persia (Iran)
1819:	Birth of the Bab in Shiraz in the south of Persia
1844:	Declaration by the Bab of his mission in the city of Shiraz
1844:	Baha'u'llah accepts the claim of the Bab and becomes a Babi (follower of the Bab)
1846:	The Bab moves to Isfahan
1847:	The Bab imprisoned in north-west Iran
1848:	The trial of the Bab in Tabriz
1848:	Conference of Badasht
1848-9:	Siege and eventual massacres of Babis at Shaykh Tabarsi
1850:	Siege and massacre of Babis at Nayriz and Zanjan
1850:	Execution of the Bab
1852:	Attempt on the life of the Shah; execution of many Babis. Baha'u'llah's vision, marking the start of his mission
1853:	Baha'u'llah exiled to Baghdad in Ottoman territory
1863:	Baha'u'llah declares his mission; is exiled to Istanbul and then Edirne
1868:	Baha'u'llah exiled to 'Akka in Syria (now Israel)
1873:	Baha'u'llah writes his book of laws, the Kitab-i Aqdas
1877:	Baha'u'llah moves outside the walls of 'Akka
1892:	Death of Baha'u'llah at Bahji, near 'Akka; start of the ministry of 'Abdu'l-Baha
1894:	The Baha'i Faith established in North America
1911-13:	Western journeys of 'Abdu'l-Baha
1921:	Death of 'Abdu'l-Baha; beginning of ministry of Shoghi Effendi
1923:	First national spiritual assemblies established (British Isles; Germany and Austria; India and Burma)
1937:	First detailed plan for the expansion of the Baha'i Faith given to Baha'i community of United States
1953:	Launch of first global plan for the expansion of the Baha'i Faith
1957:	Death of Shoghi Effendi
1963:	Election of the Universal House of Justice

Bibliography

Many of the works cited here can be found at http://www.reference.bahai.org

'Abdu'l-Bahá (1945) *Foundations of World Unity*, Wilmette, IL: Bahá'í Publishing Trust.

___ (1967) *Paris Talks*, London: Bahá'í Publishing Trust.

___ (1982) *The Promulgation of Universal Peace*, Wilmette, IL: Bahá'í Publishing Trust.

___ (1978) *Selections from the Writings of 'Abdu'l-Bahá*, Haifa: Bahá'í World Centre.

___ (1990) *The Secret of Divine Civilization*, Wilmette, IL: Bahá'í Publishing Trust.

___ (1981) *Some Answered Questions*, Wilmette, IL: Bahá'í Publishing Trust.

___ (1930) *Tablets of Abdul-Baha Abbas*, New York: Bahá'í Publishing Committee, vol. 3.

___ (1980) *A Traveler's Narrative*, Wilmette, IL: Bahá'í Publishing Trust.

___ (1891) *A Traveller's Narrative* (trans. E.G. Browne), Cambridge: Cambridge University Press, vol. 2.

___ (1991) *The Will and Testament of 'Abdu'l-Bahá*, Wilmette, IL: Bahá'í Publishing Trust.

'Abdu'l-Bahá in London (1982) London: Bahá'í Publishing Trust.

The Báb (1976) *Selections from the Writings of the Báb*, Haifa: Bahá'í World Centre.

Bahá'í International Community (for all Bahá'í International Community documents see http://www.bic-un.bahai.org/index.cfm)

___ (1947) 'A Bahá'í Declaration of Human Obligations and Rights' to the first session of the United Nations Commission on Human Rights in Lake Success, New York, February.

___ (2001b) 'Belief and Tolerance: "Lights Amidst the Darkness". Statement of the Bahá'í International Community to the International Consultative Conference on School Education in relation with Freedom of Religion and Belief, Tolerance and Non-discrimination.' Madrid, Spain, 23-5 November.

___ (1993) 'Development, Democracy and Human Rights'. Statement to the United Nations World Conference on Human Rights. Vienna, Austria, 14-25 June.

___ (1992) *Equality and the Girl Child*, BIC Document No. 92-0317, 17 March.

___ (2001a) *HIV/AIDS and Gender Equality*, June.

___ (1995a) *The Prosperity of Humankind*. New York: Bahá'í International Community United Nations Office.

___ (1995b) *Turning Point for All Nations: A Statement of the Bahá'í International Community on the Occasion of the 50th Anniversary of the United Nations*. New York: Bahá'í International Community United Nations Office.

___ (1996a) *Sustainable Communities in an Integrating World*. A statement presented to the United Nations Conference on Human Settlements (Habitat II), Istanbul, Turkey, 3B14 June, BIC Document no. 96B0530.

___ (1996b) 'Sustainable Communities in a Globalizing World', A statement presented to the Plenary of the Second UN Conference on Human Settlements (Habitat II), Istanbul, Turkey, 7 June.

___ (1998) *Valuing Spirituality in Development: Initial Considerations Regarding the Creation of Spiritually Based Indicators for Development.* London: Bahá'í Publishing Trust, 1998. A concept paper presented to the 'World Faiths and Development Dialogue' hosted by the President of the World Bank and the Archbishop of Canterbury at Lambeth Palace, London, 18B19 February. www.bic-un.bahai.org/ 98-0218.htm (accessed 1 June 2005)

Bahá'í Prayers: A Selection of Prayers revealed by Bahá'u'lláh, the Báb and 'Abdu'l-Bahá (2002) Wilmette, IL: Bahá'í Publishing Trust.

Bahá'í World Faith (1976) Wilmette, IL: Bahá'í Publishing Trust, 2nd edn.

Bahá'u'lláh (1988a) *Epistle to the Son of the Wolf*, Wilmette, IL: Bahá'í Publishing Trust.

___ (1983) *Gleanings from the Writings of Bahá'u'lláh*, Wilmette, IL: Bahá'í Publishing Trust.

___ (1990) *The Hidden Words*, Wilmette, IL: Bahá'í Publishing Trust.

___ (1992) *The Kitáb-i-Aqdas*, Haifa: Bahá'í World Centre.

___ (1989) *Kitáb-i-Íqán*, Wilmette, IL: Bahá'í Publishing Trust.

___ (1988b) *Tablets of Bahá'u'lláh.* Wilmette, IL: Bahá'í Publishing Trust.

The Compilation of Compilations (1991) Prepared by the Universal House of Justice 1963–1990. 2 vols. [Mona Vale NSW]: Bahá'í Publications Australia.

Copenhagen Declaration (1995) Annex I, para, 3. 19 April 1995, UN doc. A/Conf. 166/9.

Dawn of a New Day: Messages to India 1923–1957 (1970) New Delhi: Bahá'í Publishing Trust.

Directives from the Guardian (1973) Compiled by Gertrude Garrida. New Delhi: Bahá'í Publishing Trust.

Habitat Agenda, Chapter I B Preamble, para. 4.

Hatcher, William (2002) *Minimalism: A Bridge between Classical Philosophy and the Baha'i Revelation*, Hong Kong: Juxta Publishing, 2002.

Japan Will Turn Ablaze (1974) Japan: Bahá'í Publishing Trust.

Kassindja, Fuaziya, and Miller Bashir, Layli (1998) *Do They Hear You When You Cry?* New York: Delta.

Lights of Guidance: A Bahá'í Reference File (1997) Compiled by Helen Hornby. New Delhi: Bahá'í Publishing Trust, 5th edn.

Lucas, Mary L. (1905) *A Brief Account of My Visit to Acca*, Chicago: Baha'i Publishing Society.

Momen, Wendi (1989) *A Basic Bahá'í Dictionary*, Oxford: George Ronald.

Shoghi Effendi (1990) *The Advent of Divine Justice*, Wilmette, IL: Bahá'í Publishing Trust.

___ (1968) *Bahá'í Administration*, Wilmette, IL: Bahá'í Publishing Trust.

___ (1965) *Citadel of Faith: Messages to America 1947–1957*, Wilmette, IL: Bahá'í Publishing Trust.

___ (1970) *Dawn of a New Day: Messages to India 1923–1957*, New Delhi: Bahá'í Publishing Trust.

___ (1995) *God Passes By*, Wilmette, IL: Bahá'í Publishing Trust, rev. edn.

___ (1982) *The Light of Divine Guidance: The Messages from the Guardian of the Bahá'í Faith to the Bahá'ís of Germany and Austria*, 2 vols. Hofheim-Langenhain: Bahá'í-Verlag.

___ (1971) *Messages to the Bahá'í World*, Wilmette, IL: Bahá'í Publishing Trust.

___ (1980) *The Promised Day is Come*, Wilmette, IL: Bahá'í Publishing Trust, rev. edn.

___ (1991) *The World Order of Bahá'u'lláh*, Wilmette, IL: Bahá'í Publishing Trust.

Star of the West (1984) rpt. Oxford: George Ronald: vol. 5, no. 8 (August 1914); vol. 9, no. 3 (28 April 1918).

Training Institutes (1998): A document prepared for and approved by the Universal House of Justice, April.

United Kingdom, National Spiritual Assembly of the (2002) 'Social Cohesion: Dwelling in the Same Land', Statement by the Bahá'í Community of the United Kingdom, May.

The Universal House of Justice (1972) *The Constitution of the Universal House of Justice*, Haifa: Bahá'í World Centre.

___ (1985c) *The Promise of World Peace*. London: Bahá'í Publishing Trust, 1985.

Younghusband, Sir Francis (1923). *The Gleam*. London: John Murray.

Individual letters of Shoghi Effendi

___ (1922) to the National Spiritual Assembly of Iran, 15 February.

___ (1926) to Local Spiritual Assemblies of Iran, 30 January.

___ (1932) on behalf of Shoghi Effendi to an individual, 27 May.

___ (1933a) on behalf of Shoghi Effendi to an individual 11 August.

___ (1933b) on behalf of Shoghi Effendi to the National Spiritual Assembly of the United States and Canada, 18 November.

___ (1934) on behalf of Shoghi Effendi to an individual, 17 March.

___ (1935a) on behalf of Shoghi Effendi to an individual, 4 February.

___ (1935b) on behalf of Shoghi Effendi to an individual, 23 May.

___ (1935c) on behalf of Shoghi Effendi to two individuals, 15 November.

___ (1936a) on behalf of Shoghi Effendi to the National Spiritual Assembly of the United States, 10 January.

___ (1936b) on behalf of Shoghi Effendi to an individual, 8 March.

___ (1938) on behalf of Shoghi Effendi to an individual, 5 September.

___ (1939a) on behalf of Shoghi Effendi to an individual 19 April.

___ (1939b) on behalf of Shoghi Effendi to the National Spiritual Assembly of the British Isles, 4 June.

___ (1941) on behalf of Shoghi Effendi to two individuals, 14 October.

___ (1943) to the National Spiritual Assembly of Iran, 1 July.

___ (1944) on behalf of Shoghi Effendi to an individual, 15 May.

___ (1947) on behalf of Shoghi Effendi to an individual, 23 November.

___ (1948) on behalf of Shoghi Effendi to an individual, 8 June.

___ (1949) on behalf of Shoghi Effendi, 11 April.

___ (1952a) on behalf of Shoghi Effendi, 30 August.

___ (1952b) on behalf of Shoghi Effendi to two individuals, 15 September.

___ (1954) on behalf of Shoghi Effendi to an individual believer, 18 February.

___ (1957a) on behalf of Shoghi Effendi to an individual, 22 March.

___ (1957b) on behalf of Shoghi Effendi to the National Spiritual Assembly of the United States, 21 September.

Star of the West (1984) rpt. Oxford: George Ronald: vol. 5, no. 8 (August 1914); vol. 9, no. 3 (28 April 1918).

Training Institutes (1998): A document prepared for and approved by the Universal House of Justice, April.

United Kingdom, National Spiritual Assembly of the (2002) 'Social Cohesion: Dwelling in the Same Land', Statement by the Bahá'í Community of the United Kingdom, May.

The Universal House of Justice (1972) *The Constitution of the Universal House of Justice*, Haifa: Bahá'í World Centre.

___ (1985c) *The Promise of World Peace*. London: Bahá'í Publishing Trust, 1985.

Letters of the Universal House of Justice

___ (1969) to Continental Boards of Counsellors and National Spiritual Assemblies, 1 October.

___ (1973) to the National Spiritual Assembly of Australia, 12 November.

___ (1976) on behalf of the Universal House of Justice to an individual, 27 July.

___ (1977) on behalf of the Universal House of Justice to an individual, 24 January.

___ (1978) to the National Spiritual Assembly of Italy, 9 March.

___ (1979) on behalf of the Universal House of Justice to an individual, 8 May.

___ (1982) on behalf of the Universal House of Justice to an individual, 15 June.

___ (1983) on behalf of the Universal House of Justice, 19 January.

___ (1984a) on behalf of the Universal House of Justice to the National Spiritual Assembly of Brazil, 8 May.

___ (1984b) on behalf of the Universal House of Justice to an individual, 12 July.

___ (1984c) on behalf of the Universal House of Justice to an individual, 9 August.

___ (1985a) 31 January.

___ (1985b) on behalf of the Universal House of Justice to an individual, 31 January.

___ (1985d) to all National Spiritual Assemblies, August 7.

___ (1989) to all Baha'is, 27 August.

___ (1997) to all Continental Counsellors, 18 May.

___ (2002) to the World's Religious Leaders, April.

Websites

Baha'i International Community: www.bahai.org

Baha'i Community of the UK: www.bahai.org.uk

European Bahá'í Business Forum: www.ebbf.org (accessed 2 June 2005)

Ocean of Light
www.geocities.com/oceanoflight9/Ocean2.htm (accessed 30 May 2005)

Tahirih Justice Center: www.tahirih.org (accessed 1 June 2005)

Index

teaching, the Baha'i Faith, 33, 44, 112,
  136-7, 148
Tehran, 141
terrorism, 48, 63, 65, 78, 86, 87, 92, 94
tests and difficulties, 9-11, 16, 30
thought, liberty of, 97
tobacco, 23
Tonga, 52-3
trafficking, 58, 75, 76, 94
training institutes, 69, 122, 126-7, 128, 132
Tranquillity Zone, 56-7
transformation, personal, viii, 10, 61, 62,
  121
translation, 113
A Traveller's Narrative, 144
travelling teachers, 137
tribes, 84, 87, 92
tribunal, supreme, 96
trusteeship, 68
trustworthiness, 33, 39, 45, 47, 52, 78, 79,
  118
truth, search for, 26, 29, 30, 41, 49, 131-2

Uganda, 55-6
Uganda Baha'i Institute for Development
  (UBID), 55
Ultimate Reality, 2
UNIFEM, 130, 131
UN Special Committee on Palestine, 81
United Kingdom, 56-7
United Nations, 66, 68, 70, 72, 80, 81-2,
  87, 88, 98
  Charter, 81-2
  reform of, 95
United Nations Association, 81
United Nations Children's Fund
  (UNICEF), 82, 130
United Nations Economic and Social
  Council (ECOSOC), 82
United States, 57, 96
  National Spiritual Assembly of the
    United States and Canada, 81
united world society, *see* society, united
  world
unity
  consultation creates, 118
  covenant and, 105
  in diversity, 93
  establishment of, on all levels, 18, 32,
    35, 36, 37, 50, 77
  focus of Baha'i Faith, vii, viii, 35, 77,
    84, 103, 105
  of humanity, 61, 63, 64, 67, 71, 84, 86

  in marriage, 36-7
  world, ix, 33, 46, 61, 71, 76, 88, 92
Universal House of Justice, 81, 106,
  110-11, 145
  authority of, 108
  election of, 106-7, 116, 117
  legislation of, 73, 110
  men only serve on, 117
  to promote Lesser Peace, 100
  work of, ix, 110
universities, 132-3

vaccinations, 55-6
Vahid, 140
values, 29, 36, 39, 40-1, 42, 50, 62, 66, 69,
  79, 80, 87, 95
  of Baha'i community, 103, 121, 128
  children to be trained in, 39, 52
  lack of, 78
vegetable growing, 54-5
vegetarianism, 20
veil, 139
Victoria, Queen, 142
victory, 63, 65
violence, 23, 33, 41, 48, 58, 65, 92, 131
  domestic, 64
virtues, 61, 68, 78
  teaching of, 45, 52
vision, Baha'i, of world, 4, 33, 46, 86-102
volition, 80
voluntary sharing, 25, 30
vote, the, 69
  in Baha'i consultation, 119

Waltama, Chad, 59
war, 64, 65, 69, 71, 86, 88, 92, 94-5, 99
Washington DC, 57-8
wealth, 25-6, 63
  acquisition of, 62
  extremes of, and poverty, 50, 64, 86, 94
  purification of, 135
  voluntary sharing of, 25, 30
  wealth creation, 45, 51
weapons, 95, 96, 101
weights and measures, 99, 100
WHO (World Health Organisation), 82
widows, 21, 130
will, political, 80
Will and Testament of `Abdu'l-Baha, 113,
  145
wills, 39
wisdom, 35, 56